SALADIN

LEADERSHIP ▪ STRATEGY ▪ CONFLICT

DAVID NICOLLE ▪ ILLUSTRATED BY PETER DENNIS

First published in 2011 by Osprey Publishing
Midland House, West Way, Botley, Oxford OX2 0PH, UK
44-02 23rd St, Suite 219, Long Island City, NY 11101, USA

E-mail: info@ospreypublishing.com

ISBN: 978 1 84908 317 1
E-book ISBN: 978 1 84908 318 8

Editorial by Ilios Publishing Ltd, Oxford, UK
Maps by Mapping Specialists Ltd
Page layout by Myriam Bell Design, France
Index by David Worthington
Originated by Blenheim Colour, UK
Printed in China through Worldprint Ltd

11 12 13 14 15   10 9 8 7 6 5 4 3 2 1

A CIP catalogue record for this book is available from the British Library.

www.ospreypublishing.com

Dedication

For Angus McBride and Richard Hook, the best collaborators an author could wish for.

Artist's note

Readers may care to note that the original paintings from which the colour plates in this book were prepared are available for private sale. All reproduction copyright whatsoever is retained by the Publishers. All enquiries should be addressed to:

Peter Dennis, Fieldhead, The Park, Mansfield, NG18 2AT

The Publishers regret that they can enter into no correspondence upon this matter.

The Woodland Trust

Osprey Publishing are supporting the Woodland Trust, the UK's leading woodland conservation charity, by funding the dedication of trees.

Cover image

Angus McBride © Osprey Publishing Ltd. Taken from Men-at-Arms 171: *Saladin and the Saracens*.

Back cover image

© Master and Fellows of Corpus Christi College, Cambridge.

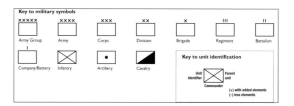

CONTENTS

INTRODUCTION

Saladin, or Yusuf Ibn Najm al-Din Ayyub Salah al-Din to give the shortened version of his proper name, lived at a time when the Islamic world was going through profound changes. Since the later 11th century Turkish ruling elites had dominated most of the Islamic Middle East. In military terms Arabs and Persians were being pushed aside, though they continued to dominate the religious, cultural and commercial elites. Meanwhile Kurds had only limited and localized importance, which makes the rise of a man of Kurdish origins like Saladin all the more unusual.

During this period the cultural centre of the Islamic world also shifted westwards from Iran and central Iraq to northern Iraq, Syria and Egypt. Baghdad, capital of the Sunni Muslim 'Abbasid Caliphate, retained its importance but was being rivalled by Mosul, Aleppo, Damascus and, after Saladin overthrew the Shia Muslim Fatimid Caliphate in Egypt, Cairo. Iran and Iraq had been the heartlands of Great Saljuq Turkish power but even here

Opposite

1 1164: Saladin accompanies Shirkuh with an army sent to the Fatimid Caliphate by Nur al-Din of Syria against King Amalric of Jerusalem's second intervention; he defeats the Fatimids at Qawn al-Rish on 18 July, but is besieged in Bilbays from August to November and withdraws to Syria.

2 1167: Saladin and Shirkuh campaign against King Amalric of Jerusalem's third intervention, defeating the Crusader–Fatimid alliance at al-Babayn on 18 March; Saladin leads the defence of Alexandria (May–June), then withdraws to Syria.

3 1169: Saladin and Shirkuh are invited to bring an army to Egypt to confront King Amalric's fifth intervention; Saladin takes over as commander of Nur al-Din's forces in Egypt after the death of Shirkuh and is appointed *wazir* of the Fatimid caliph (March); Saladin crushes a rebellion by Sudanese regiments of the Fatimid caliphal army (August) then defeats a Byzantine–Crusader siege of Dumyat (October–December).

4 1170: Saladin raids Darum and Gaza, and retakes Aylah from the Kingdom of Jerusalem (December).

5 1171: Saladin takes over as governor of Egypt on the death of the last Fatimid caliph, ruling in the name of Nur al-Din of Syria (September).

6 1171: Mosul recognizes the suzerainty of Nur al-Din.

7 1171: Aborted joint attack on Karak by Saladin and Nur al-Din (September–November).

8 1172: Nubians attack Aswan; retaliation by Saladin's brother Turan Shah installs a garrison in Qasr Ibrim (summer to December).

9 1173: Saladin leads an army against Bedouin tribes in Oultrejordain to secure a route between Egypt and Syria, then raids Karak (summer).

10 1173: Saladin sends an army under Qaraqush on its first expedition into Libya.

11 1173: Sicilian–Norman fleet attacks Alexandria (July–August).

12 1173: Pro-Fatimid rising in Upper Egypt led by Kanz al-Dawla, the governor of Aswan, is crushed by Saladin's brother al-'Adil (August–September).

13 1174: Death of Nur al-Din (15 May); Saladin takes control of Damascus, Hims and Hama (October–December).

14 1174: Saladin sends Turan Shah with an army and supporting fleet to conquer Yemen (February–June).

Saladin's rise to power (frontiers c.1171)

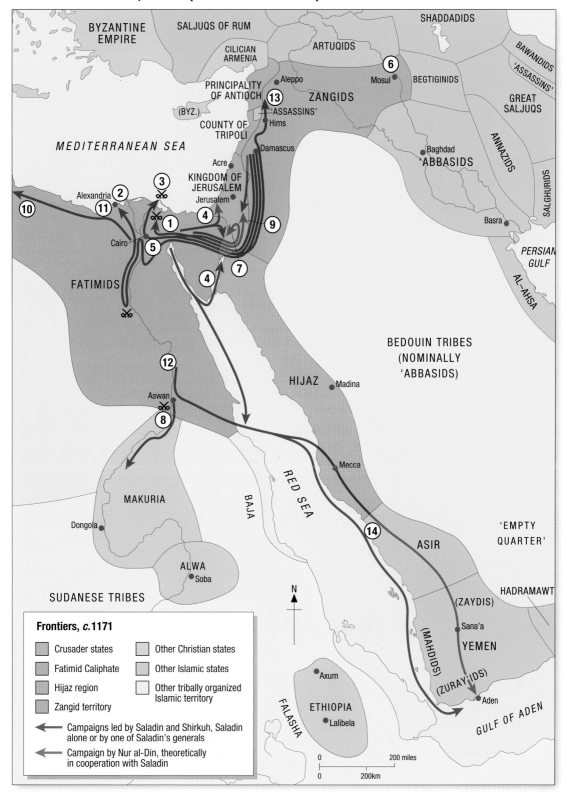

Frontiers, c.1171

- Crusader states
- Fatimid Caliphate
- Hijaz region
- Zangid territory
- Other Christian states
- Other Islamic states
- Other tribally organized Islamic territory
- Campaigns led by Saladin and Shirkuh, Saladin alone or by one of Saladin's generals
- Campaign by Nur al-Din, theoretically in cooperation with Saladin

During the Middle Ages Jazirat Ibn Umar (now Cizre in south-eastern Turkey) served as a major river port as well as a strategic crossing point over the Tigris. (Author's photograph)

the Saljuq realm would fragment shortly after Saladin's birth. In Baghdad the 'Abbasid Caliphate, having long been a pawn in the power games of other dynasties, was also beginning to re-emerge as a significant power.

To the north and west, in the Jazira (Mesopotamia) region between the Tigris and Euphrates rivers, and in most of Syria, Lebanon, Jordan, Palestine and parts of southern Turkey, Great Saljuq authority had already been replaced by that of *atabegs* ('princes' father-figures'). Indeed the *atabeg* state founded by 'Imad al-Din Zangi would itself be divided between his sons, of whom Nur al-Din inherited his father's role as the leading Muslim champion against the invading Crusaders. He would also be Saladin's patron.

The power of the Crusader states that had been established in the aftermath of the First Crusade (see Campaign 132: *The First Crusade*) was not yet broken, though the County of Edessa, the first Crusader state to be created, had been destroyed by 'Imad al-Din Zangi. Nur al-Din then retook most Crusader territory in the Orontes Valley, reducing the once-powerful Principality of Antioch to little more than a narrow coastal strip along the Mediterranean. The Crusader County of Tripoli remained virtually unchanged while the most powerful Crusader state, the Kingdom of Jerusalem, remained a potent threat with ambitions to expand eastward while also striving to dominate Egypt where the decline of the Fatimid Caliphate was now clear to all.

Of course, rulers like Saladin and Nur al-Din had to keep in mind other Christian communities within their own realms. Many parts of Syria and Egypt still had local Christian majorities, while others had substantial Christian minorities; this was also true of several parts of the Jazira. Nevertheless, most such indigenous Christians were regarded as heretics by the Crusaders. Furthermore, the Islamic civilization in which Saladin was born and brought up had several Christian states and peoples as neighbours, other than those of the European Crusaders. Cilician Armenia had forged a close alliance with the Crusader states, while Georgia was enjoying a political, military and cultural golden age. In fact, conflict between an expansionist Georgia and the Muslim rulers of Akhlat meant that the latter rarely took much interest in the struggle against the Crusaders. The Byzantine Empire was now a reduced, through still formidable, power, having recovered much of the territory lost in the later 11th century.

Saladin's primary concerns were, of course, affairs within the *umma* or community of Islam. Here tensions between the Sunni and the Shia strands of Islam were deteriorating rapidly. Today Shia form a majority only in most of Iran, plus southern and parts of central Iraq, though there are also significant Shia communities in Syria, Lebanon and Yemen. Before the mid-12th century, however, the size of Shia Muslim, Christian, Jewish and other communities meant that supposedly mainstream Sunni Muslims actually formed a minority in many parts of Egypt and Syria. It is therefore no exaggeration to state that the revival of Sunni 'orthodoxy'

'Jason the Hero' in a copy of al-Sufi's *Book of Stars* made within a few years of Saladin's birth, probably in Egypt. (Topkapi Library, Ms. Ahmad III, 3493, f.30r, Istanbul)

A

B

C

By Saladin's lifetime the mace came in a variety of forms, ranging from the animal-headed *gurz* (A) to the flanged *dabbus* (B) and elongated *latt* (C). (A – Furusiyya Art Foundation, London; B – private collection, Israel; C – Museum of Islamic Art, Cairo)

The men shown on this 12th-century Kashan-ware moulded jar from Iran are dancing in the same manner that can be seen across most of the Islamic Middle East to this day. (Private collection)

championed by leaders like Nur al-Din and Saladin was aimed at least as much against the Shia as it was against the invading Crusaders.

To understand the strengths and the weaknesses of Saladin's position it is necessary to look at the theoretical basis of his authority. The medieval Middle East was an arena where religious law rather than military power ultimately decided whether a dynasty could maintain itself. Here, perhaps even more than in medieval Europe, an ambitious ruler needed the acquiescence of his people and the support of religious or legal as well as military elites if he was to achieve anything.

During the late 11th to early 13th centuries Sunni Muslim scholars reinterpreted the role of the Sunni caliph as imam or spiritual leader of the Muslim community. Most day-to-day power lay in the hands of sultans, but rulership was defined as a partnership between a sultan and the caliph. Nevertheless, there could be no legal separation of 'church and state' in societies firmly based upon Islamic law. What a scholar like al-Ghazali outlined was a system where the sultan carried on the business of government, but only if his authority was formally recognized by the 'Abbasid caliph. Unfortunately, the current caliphs of Baghdad, while still being the spiritual leaders of Sunni Islam, were also becoming militarily significant rulers. From Saladin's point of view, the scope for 'Abbasid interference remained a problem, especially as he was himself widely regarded as an usurper who had turned against the sons of his master, Nur al-Din. Hence the importance of Saladin's fight against the Crusaders as a way of legitimizing himself as the strongest ruler in the Middle East.

CHRONOLOGY

1138   Birth of Saladin (Yusuf ibn Ayyub) at Tikrit; his family flees to 'Imad al-Din Zangi of Mosul.

1154   Saladin's father Ayyub and uncle Shirkuh in the service of Nur al-Din of Damascus, where Saladin spends his formative years.

1164   Saladin accompanies his uncle Shirkuh on a campaign to the Fatimid Caliphate of Egypt.

1167	Saladin leads defence of Alexandria against a Crusader–Fatimid alliance.
1169	Saladin takes command of Nur al-Din's forces in Egypt after the death of his uncle Shirkuh; he is appointed *wazir* (vizier) of the Fatimid Caliphate, which still rules Egypt.
1171	Saladin becomes governor of Egypt on the death of the last Fatimid caliph, ruling in the name of Nur al-Din of Syria.
1173–75	Saladin sends forces to raid Nubia.
1174	Death of Nur al-Din; Saladin begins campaigns to dominate what had been Nur al-Din's domains, taking Damascus, Hims and Hama in central Syria; Saladin sends an army to conquer Yemen.
1175–76	Saladin campaigns against Nur al-Din's successor in northern Syria and sends forces to control north-eastern Libya; attempts to dominate territory further west are thwarted by the Muwahhidun.
1177	Saladin's raid into the Crusader Kingdom of Jerusalem is defeated at Tall al-Safiya.
1179	Saladin defeats the Kingdom of Jerusalem at Marj al-'Uyun.
1181	Reynald of Châtillon raids north-western Arabia.
1182	Saladin raids the Kingdom of Jerusalem; Reynald of Châtillon sends a raiding fleet into the Red Sea.
1183	Reynald of Châtillon's Red Sea fleet is defeated; Saladin raids the Kingdom of Jerusalem, and also takes control of Aleppo, Mayyafariqin, Mardin and Amida (Diyarbakir) while Mosul in northern Iraq recognizes his indirect suzerainty.
1187	Reynald of Châtillon attacks a Muslim Pilgrimage caravan; Saladin defeats the Kingdom of Jerusalem at Hattin and retakes almost all of it, including Jerusalem.
1188–89	Saladin continues to retake Crusader territory with the exceptions of Tyre (Sur), Tripoli and Antioch.
1189	Third Crusade is launched in Western Europe; forces of the Kingdom of Jerusalem advance from Tyre to besiege Acre; Saladin then besieges the besiegers.
1191	Third Crusade takes Acre; Saladin fails to stop them at Arsuf.
1192	Saladin defeats Crusader attempts to reach Jerusalem; the Crusader leader King Richard of England makes peace with Saladin and returns home.
1193	Saladin dies on 3 March.

On of the few palatial reception halls to survive from around Saladin's lifetime still stands right on the bank of the great river Tigris in Mosul, northern Iraq. (Author's photograph)

THE EARLY YEARS

Saladin is usually described as being a Kurd, but while this might be true of his paternal family origins, it is misleading. The young Yusuf Ibn Ayyub, the future Saladin, was brought up in a largely Turkish military community in an Arabic-speaking Syrian urban environment, while the Kurdishness of his immediate family was a matter of ethnic origin rather than culture. His father Ayyub and his uncle Shirkuh had the biggest influence upon his early life and they were certainly not uncultured mountain tribesmen. Instead they stemmed from the aristocracy of Dvin in what is now Armenia. They served powerful Arab and Turkish rulers in Iraq and Syria where they and their relations formed part of an elite of military families. Nevertheless they were not amongst the most powerful.

The Roman temple complex of Baalbak was made into an important citadel during the Crusades. Saladin spent much of his childhood in this frontier fortress. (Author's photograph)

Saladin was actually born in the central Iraqi city of Tikrit in 1138, his father and uncle being military governors on behalf of the Great Saljuq Sultan Muhammad Ibn Malik Shah. Although Tikrit was an important posting with a substantial citadel it was more significant as a centre of Christian and Muslim scholarship. However, Saladin was less than a year old when Shirkuh was accused of murder and the family had to flee. Ayyub and Shirkuh next found employment in the army of 'Imad al-Din Zangi, the *atabeg* of Mosul. Thereafter Saladin's childhood was relatively stable. From 1139 his father Ayyub governed the exposed frontier town of Baalbak in Lebanon, but when Zangi was assassinated in 1146 the ruler of Damascus sent an army to retake Baalbak. Ayyub agreed to surrender if he was allowed to remain governor, and as a sweetener he was offered an *'iqta* fief of ten villages near Damascus plus a fine house in the city.

Unfortunately this placed Ayyub and his brother Shirkuh in opposing camps because Shirkuh remained loyal to Zangi's son and heir Nur al-Din. Meanwhile, the young Saladin grew up in the cultured environment of Damascus where he was educated as a young gentleman and a future member of the governing class. Most of what is known about such education focuses on religion, ethics and culture, rather than practical skills. But by the 12th century the *hadiths* or 'traditions' of the Prophet Muhammad's life had been formulated into a teaching discipline, grouped under topics that covered most aspects of life including government and warfare. According to Zaki al-Din al-Wahrani, a North African scholar who was supposedly quoting Saladin, the ideal education of a scholar should also include archery and the use of weapons. Saladin's sons are known to have ridden, played polo and practised archery outside the Citadel of Damascus every evening, so it is almost certain that Saladin had done the same.

Saladin maintained that he learned about justice and rulership from Nur al-Din and insisted that his own conduct merely continued that of his illustrious predecessor. The evidence certainly shows that Saladin learned how to conduct effective propaganda warfare against rival Muslim rulers during his campaigns to unite the Muslim Middle East against the 'Frankish' Crusaders. In fact Saladin spent some 16 years in Nur al-Din's service, in administrative as well as military roles.

In no way was the young Saladin the quiet subordinate who unwillingly took over his uncle Shirkuh's position in Egypt in 1169, as described by romantic 19th-century historians. A more accurate statement is that of a 12th-century scholar who is said to have told Saladin: 'As for the jihad, you are the nursling of its milk and the child of its bosom. Gird up therefore the shanks of spears to meet it, and plunge on in its service into a sea of sword-points.'[1]

Many different forms of hunting were enjoyed by the ruling and military elites of Saladin's period. The most aristocratic was hawking, as shown on this 12th-century Egyptian lustre-ware plate. It was from the Middle East that the Western European knightly class learned this sport. (Freer Gallery of Art, Washington; author's photograph)

When Saladin was sent to Egypt in 1164 as part of the army commanded by his uncle Shirkuh he was certainly no novice. Instead he was recognized as a competent, trustworthy and ambitious leader. This expedition was Nur al-Din's first direct military intervention in the affairs of the rapidly crumbling Fatimid Caliphate and was intended to forestall Crusader domination of Egypt. In military terms it was a failure, but in 1167 Nur al-Din sent another army with essentially the same command structure. This time the Syrians defeated a combined Crusader–Fatimid army at the battle of al-Babayn in Upper Egypt on 18 April. It was Saladin's first experience of a full-scale battle. However, the enemy rapidly regrouped and within a few weeks the 28-year-old Saladin found himself commanding the defence of the great seaport of Alexandria with 1,000 cavalry, plus the army's sick and wounded.

This siege lasted from early May until early August but a truce was eventually agreed upon and the Syrians left Egypt. In October 1168 King Amalric marched into Egypt again, sacking Bilbays and threatening Cairo itself. The third expedition that Nur al-Din sent to Egypt in response to this Crusader assault was much more successful and took control of the country, though still under the nominal authority of the Fatimid caliph. Shirkuh was even appointed as the caliph's chief *wazir* but then, in his moment of triumph, Saladin's uncle suddenly died in March 1169. This threatened a serious crisis

1   Partner, G., *God of Battles: Holy Wars of Christianity and Islam* (Princeton, 1997) p. 93.

Al-Babayn, 18 or 19 March 1167

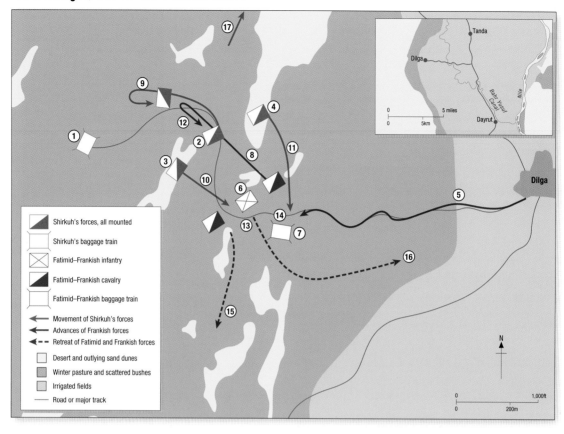

1 Shirkuh's baggage train between the main desert and the sand hills.

2 Saladin almost certainly in command of the centre, largely consisting of Arab Bedouin troops, with orders to fall back towards the baggage train and then to counter-attack as the situation allowed.

3 Shirkuh probably in command of the traditionally offensive right wing, largely consisting of Turkish Ghuzz troops including Shirkuh's own Asadiyah personal regiment.

4 The traditionally defensive left wing, including or largely consisting of Kurdish troops under an unnamed commander.

5 Fatimid–Frankish army arrives from al-Ushmunayn, having crossed the Bahr Yusuf canal east of Dilga.

6 Fatimid–Frankish array probably with Frankish cavalry under Hughes of Caesara on the right, Fatimid cavalry under the *wazir* Shawar on the left and a mixed Fatimid and Frankish infantry and cavalry centre under King Amalric.

7 Fatimid–Frankish baggage train.

8 Frankish cavalry under Hughes of Caesarea attacks the enemy's centre, perhaps believing it to be commanded by Shirkuh.

9 The centre under Saladin falls back towards Shirkuh's baggage train, then counter-attacks after Shirkuh charges the main enemy line.

10 Shirkuh and the right wing close the gap behind Hughes of Caesarea and attack the main Fatimid–Frankish position.

11 Shirkuh's left wing probably also charges, perhaps heading for the enemy's baggage train.

12 Frankish cavalry under Hughes of Caesarea suffer severe losses, Hughes himself being captured while most of the knights probably flee.

13 The main Fatimid–Frankish force crumbles and abandons the field; Hugues of Creona and Eustache Cholet are killed while Arnulf of Tall Bashir and Bishop Raoul of Bethlehem are captured.

14 The Fatimid–Frankish baggage train is captured.

15 Scattered fighting continues in 'valleys' south of the battlefield.

16 Amalric rallies his men while the nearest enemy troops are preoccupied with other targets; he retreats across the Bahr Yusuf and then to Minyat Ibn al-Khasib (now al-Minya); Shawar probably retreats in the same direction and they are joined by Gerard of Pongi, Jocelin of Samosata and perhaps Shawar's son al-Kamil with the largely infantry force that has crossed the Nile.

17 Shirkuh's army returns north, keeping the Bahr Yusuf canal between themselves and the main enemy force.

for the Syrian expeditionary force and for Nur al-Din's influence in Egypt. It was necessary to chose a new leader from the officers on the spot, and the man the army selected was Saladin.

When Saladin was appointed as the Fatimid caliphs' chief *wazir* in Shirkuh's place, he also became commander of the Fatimid army. In fact there had for many years been two Fatimid armies – one commanded and recruited directly by the *wazirs*, and a separate corps of palace regiments owing allegiance directly to the Fatimid caliph. Unfortunately Saladin faced opposition from both. Meanwhile the last Fatimid caliph, the young and sickly al-'Adid, did not expect his dynasty to be overthrown and his relationship with Saladin appeared friendly. Nevertheless, within a year Saladin was reducing the power and influence of Shia Islam within the state while at the same time skilfully using various elements of the Fatimid state system to consolidate his own power.

THE MILITARY LIFE

By the time the ailing al-'Adid, last caliph of the Fatimid dynasty, died during the early hours of Monday 13 September 1171, he had neither real power nor even religious authority within Egypt. Saladin could now concentrate upon strengthening Egypt as a bastion of Sunni Muslim power with himself as governor in the name of Nur al-Din of Syria. However, tension between Saladin and Nur al-Din soon emerged and had almost resulted in conflict when Nur al-Din also suddenly died in May 1174.

The main reason for this deteriorating relationship was financial. Nur al-Din saw Egypt as something of a cash cow whose resources could finance his own expanding military machine in Syria. Meanwhile Saladin wanted to build up Egyptian strength, and thus his own, as another major military power capable of taking on the Crusader states. Nevertheless, Saladin was soon governing and campaigning beyond his means. This would remain a serious problem even after his victory at Hattin in 1187. In the meantime he knew that the old Fatimid army, though increasing in efficiency, was not necessarily becoming more loyal to Saladin's new regime. So he withheld the revenues that Nur al-Din was expecting, and used much of them to expand the expeditionary force that Shirkuh had brought to Egypt, creating an army loyal to himself alone. Saladin's armies in Egypt and later in Syria and northern Iraq have been studied for over a century, but many misconceptions remain. Despite Saladin's Kurdish origins, Turks dominated the new army. Kurds were also prominent but remained secondary.

After 'liberating the Hajj Road' by recapturing Aylah and therefore enabling Muslim pilgrims from Spain, North Africa and Egypt to travel in safety to the Islamic holy places in Arabia, Saladin did remarkably little to justify his self-proclaimed role as a leader of the jihad. In fact until 1187 the majority of his campaigns were against fellow Muslim rulers. This policy eventually established a virtually united front against the Crusader states, but in the

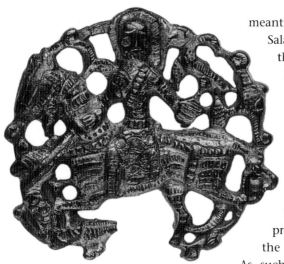

A horseman with a hawk upon his wrist is illustrated on this gilded bronze harness decoration. Dating from the 12th or early 13th century it was made in Syria or what is now central Turkey. (Furusiyya Art Foundation, London)

meantime it led to considerable criticism. For example, Saladin sent armies westwards into North Africa where they clashed with the rising power of the Moroccan Muwahhidun dynasty. By dominating this area Saladin hoped to control piracy and recruited personnel for his revived Egyptian fleet, but beyond the province of Barqa (Cyrenaica) in eastern Libya Saladin's authority was never consolidated.

Saladin's campaigns southwards had similarly strategic aims, the main targets being Nubia in the Nile Valley and Yemen at the southern tip of the Arabian Peninsula. Both were hotbeds of pro-Fatimid and Isma'ili support, despite the fact that the kingdoms of Nubia were still officially Christian. As such, both were a danger to Saladin. At the time of Saladin's takeover, the situation in the frontier zone between the northernmost Nubian kingdom and Egypt was anarchic. The threat came not only from Nubians but also from black *sudani* Africans, who almost certainly included ex-Fatimid soldiers and survivors of the uprising against Saladin back in 1169. As confusion spread across southern Egypt, Kanz al-Dawla, the tribal leader who was nominally in charge of the area, asked Saladin, the new master of Cairo, for help. Eventually Saladin sent his ruthless half-brother Turan Shah to expel the Nubians and *sudani*. Then in 1174 Kanz al-Dawla himself rose in revolt in the name of the Fatimids and joined forces with Christian Nubians. This time the outcome was more decisive, with Kanz al-Dawla being killed just as he was preparing to march against Cairo. Thereafter things remained relatively stable for over a century, during which the Nubian kingdoms witnessed a remarkable final flowering of Christian Sudanese civilization.

Yemen posed a danger as a source of pro-Fatimid plots, much of the country having been ruled by an Isma'ili Shia dynasty known as the Sulayhids from 1047 to 1138. Strategically Yemen was even more important because it controlled the eastern side of the Bab al-Mandib Straits linking Egypt with India, east Africa and the Far East. Naval warfare was a very rare occurrence in these eastern seas compared to the situation in the Mediterranean but there was a continuing danger of piracy.

Hence Saladin's decision to dominate Yemen was to consolidate Muslim control over the entire Red Sea while protecting the maritime pilgrimage route from Egypt and the Sudan to the Islamic holy cities of Mecca and Madina in Arabia. The first expedition he sent to Yemen early in 1174 included a few ships but was primarily an overland march and was again commanded by Saladin's ambitious brother, Turan Shah. The rarity of naval warfare, and thus of real warships, had been a feature of these eastern seas for millennia, but things changed for a while following Saladin's conquest of Yemen. A small number of war galleys of the type known as *shinis* were transported from the Nile to the Red Sea and thence to the vital Yemeni port of Aden. However, these galleys then sat unused for years. Quite what these galleys were doing when the Crusader fleet sent by Reynald of Châtillon spread mayhem around the Red Sea in 1183 is unrecorded.

Nur al-Din's death in 1174 opened up the possibility of Saladin taking over much of the Middle East as Nur al-Din's inheritor. In fact he could not intervene immediately because a Sicilian Norman fleet was threatening the Egyptian coast, but once this danger passed and Kanz al-Dawla's uprising in southern Egypt was crushed, Saladin proclaimed the need for unity and jihad as a justification for intervening in Syria. Generally speaking Saladin found more support amongst ordinary people and lower-ranking soldiers than he did amongst senior personnel, both civilian and military, during his campaigns to take over from Nur al-Din's descendants and other members of the Zangid dynasty in Syria, the Jazira and northern Iraq. Yet even after winning control of Damascus in October 1174 Saladin remained merely 'governor' of Egypt and southern Syria. Not until the following year was he recognized as sultan or senior ruler of the region.

Aleppo was more difficult to take and Saladin had to fight real campaigns before northern Syria fell under his control. Here and in northern Iraq the Zangid rulers regarded him as a Kurdish upstart who had turned against the family of his employer. So Saladin used his self-proclaimed position as leader of the jihad against the Crusader states to undermine support for these Zangid rivals. In military terms his operations against these fellow Muslims were mostly on a small scale. Politically he was more brutal, and succeeded in winning over various smaller dynasties that already resented Zangid pretentions.

There were more sieges than field battles during Saladin's conquest of these Islamic provinces, some of which were very ruthless. That of Manbij is worthy of note and began on 11 May 1176. The place was actually held by Qutb al-Din Yinal ibn Hassan al-Manbiji, whom the chronicler Ibn al-Athir described as a fierce enemy of Saladin. Eventually Saladin became so exasperated that he seized the town of Manbij, 'but the citadel remained, held by its lord (Qutb al-Din Yinal) who had gathered there men, weapons and stores. Saladin besieged him and pressed him hard, carrying out assaults on the citadel. The sappers reached the wall, mined it and the place was taken by storm. Saladin's troops took everything within as booty. Saladin took its lord Yinal prisoner and took all his wealth, leaving him poor, not possessing a bean.'[2]

Criticism of Saladin, claiming he spent more effort attacking fellow Muslims than he did on jihad against the Crusader states, was only partially justified. As early as 1177 Saladin led a large-scale raid into the Kingdom of Jerusalem, probably to forestall a feared Crusader–Byzantine assault on Egypt following the arrival of a crusade led by Philip of Flanders. In fact Saladin's counter-strike was almost a disaster, culminating in defeat at Tall al-Safiya

A carved, but also charred, 12th-century wooden plaque showing a warrior-saint equipped in the Middle Eastern rather than Byzantine style, from the northern Nubian capital of Old Dongola. (Sudan National Museum, inv. no. D.1/98, Khartoum; Wojciech Chmiel photograph)

---

2 Ibn al-Athir (tr. Richards, D. S.), *The Chronicle of Ibn al-Athir for the Crusading Period, part 2: The Years 541–589/1146–1193* (Aldershot, 2007) pp. 242–43.

A number of raids into southern Egypt by the Christian Kingdom of Nubia led to counter-attacks by Saladin's forces, which reached as far as the ancient Nubian capital of Dongola. (Author's photograph)

(Mont Gisard) on 25 November. Reynald of Châtillon, the new lord of Oultrejordain in what is now southern Jordan, was largely responsible for Saladin's discomfiture and the battle of Tall al-Safiya was just one in a series of increasingly personal clashes between himself and Saladin.

Many in Saladin's army were taken prisoner at Tall al-Safiya but only the most senior are known to have been ransomed. Very little is known about the fate of lower-ranking captives, so a letter sent by one such man to friends or family in Egypt is particularly interesting. It survived amongst other documents in the *geniza* or 'hiding place' in the Ben Ezra synagogue in Cairo. Since the writer was captured by the Kingdom of Jerusalem between 1174 and 1187, the battle of Tall al-Safiya was the most likely occasion. His name is unknown but he clearly feared being forgotten about for not being an important person.[3]

Two years later Saladin achieved a significant victory – he not only defeated a Frankish force at Marj al-'Ayun but then took over a new Crusader castle overlooking the strategic Jacob's Ford crossing point over the upper river Jordan. Nevertheless this campaign was very expensive at a time when Saladin's government was already short of money. So the two-year truce that was subsequently agreed probably came as a relief to both sides, especially as the effects of a severe drought and the resulting famine added to the destruction of crops during the campaign itself. This drought lasted five years and was particularly severe in Damascus, where the city and the surrounding Ghuta oasis were entirely dependent upon a sophisticated system of canals that took drinking, drainage and irrigation water from the small river Barada.

Egypt had the mighty Nile, which rises deep in Africa and consequently escaped this particular climatic crisis. Indeed, the importance of caravan convoys of food supplies from Egypt to Syria during these years is hard

---

3 Cahen, C., 'Une lettre d'un prisonnier musulman des Francs de Syrie', in (ed. anon.), *Études de civilization médiévale (IXe-XIe siècle): Mélanges offerts à Edmond-René Labande* (Poitiers, 1975) pp. 83–87.

Saladin brings his brother Turan Shah to the Fatimid Caliphate capital of Cairo with an army, August 1169

Saladin, newly appointed as chief *wazir* to the young Fatimid Caliph al-'Adid, invited his elder brother Shams al-Dawla Turan Shah to join him in Cairo. However, Turan Shah not only brought his family and retinue but also a substantial army provided by Saladin's sovereign, Nur al-Din of Syria. Although the 19-year-old Caliph al-'Adid, a sickly youth who would die only two years later, welcomed Turan Shah as a friend, many in the Fatimid court saw these newcomers as strengthening Saladin's position while weakening their own. One of the most worried was the caliph's close advisor, the Nubian eunuch al-Mu'tamin al-Khilafah, who was a close ally of the Fatimid *'abid* guard regiments recruited from Sudanese slaves.

Rashid al-Din Sinan ruled an Isma'ili mini-state that effectively defied all comers. His tomb outside Masyaf is still a place of importance to Isma'ilis. (Author's photograph)

to overstate. Since Saladin had freed the Hajj Road by retaking Aylah, such caravans did not have to pass through Crusader territory. Nevertheless they remained vulnerable to Reynald of Châtillon's fief of Oultrejordain and its castle garrisons, which could still threaten communications between Egypt and Syria. Further north a spur of Crusader territory along the lower part of the river Yarmouk, centred upon the remarkable cave-fortress of Habis Jaldak, posed similar dangers.

As Lord of Oultrejordain, Reynald cultivated good relations with several Bedouin Arab tribes. Chroniclers generally described the latter as predatory, mercenary and as traitors to Islam. In reality many of them had deep grievances and fundamental religious disagreements with Saladin and with many of the other largely Turkish ruling elites of the Islamic Middle East. Reynald's first raid was a sudden assault upon a large caravan at the oasis of Tayma, 400km south of Karak, during the winter of 1181–82 when grass was available for the raiders' horses. Like all Reynald campaigns, it had a sound strategic objective, diverting Saladin's attention away from Aleppo in northern Syria and thus delaying his unification of the lands surrounding the Crusader states.

His next operation was the even more daring Red Sea raid of the winter of 1182–83, though he did not himself take part. Reynald's ships were built by Syrian Christians, probably on the Mediterranean coast rather than mountainous Oultrejordain. They were then taken as prefabricated pieces to be launched in the Gulf of Aqaba. The Crusader warlord was, in fact, copying what Saladin had done when he retook Crusader-held Aqaba a decade earlier. The resulting naval operation not only had a huge psychological impact by attacking the Muslims' Red Sea pilgrimage routes and threatening Islam's holiest sites, but it also interrupted trade between Egypt and India.

In 1183 Saladin decided he was strong enough to launch a major raid into the Kingdom of Jerusalem, but it again failed. Saladin's efforts farther north, in the fertile hills now known as the Jabal Ajlun, were more successful and in 580 AH (1184–85) Saladin ordered an amir named 'Izz al-Din to move from his current post as governor of the frontier hills behind Beirut to take over Ajlun. Both areas held important iron mines, so perhaps 'Izz al-Din was a specialist in these matters.

Saladin was at least as skilled a diplomat as he was a military commander and his broad strategic vision led him to cultivate good relations with the Byzantine Empire. Both states wanted to contain the Saljuq Sultanate of Rum in what is now central Turkey, though Saladin had to proceed with caution because the Saljuqs could serve as useful allies against the Crusader Principality of Antioch. His task was made easier by a shattering defeat suffered by the

Byzantines at the hands of the Saljuqs at Myriokephalon in 1176. The death of the pro-Crusader Emperor Manuel in 1180 was then followed by increasing tension between the Orthodox Greek Byzantines and their Latin Catholic neighbours. A golden opportunity came when two senior members of the Byzantine aristocracy, Isaac and Alexius Angelus, fled to Syria as refugees from Emperor Andronicus (r. 1183–85). Saladin cultivated their friendship until Isaac returned home in 1185 to become the new Byzantine Emperor. It was a bonus when, hearing rumours of an alliance between Isaac and Saladin, the Crusader Count of Tripoli took Alexius Angelus prisoner as he was on his way home to Constantinople some months later.

THE HOUR OF DESTINY

Saladin's invasion of the Crusader Kingdom of Jerusalem in 1187 differed little from some previous incursions. Western historians have tended to describe it as a massive attempt to crush the Franks by a huge army, but in reality even at the height of Saladin's power the Crusader states could field an army equal in size to his own, in many ways better equipped and similarly well disciplined. The fall of the Kingdom of Jerusalem was in no sense inevitable and Saladin may have been more nervous of the outcome of this particular campaign than his opponents were. His weak control over an extended 'empire' meant that defeat or even a setback could prove politically disastrous. On the other hand a successful raid would help to consolidate Saladin's position vis-à-vis rival Muslim leaders.

Whether Saladin anticipated a major battle in 1187 is also unclear. The army that he led on this campaign was mixed, including armed and unarmoured cavalry, large numbers of infantry and siege equipment. Such evidence suggests that the incursion was intended to be more than another case of economically damaging 'ravaging' warfare.

Behind the battlefront, the year 1187 saw Saladin's government seek to strengthen its position in other ways. This included major financial reforms which, though less dramatic than events in Palestine, did include an effort to remove debased currency from circulation. It had only a temporary impact and the problem of debased currency would subsequently grow worse during the Third Crusade. Here it is interesting to note that, just as special taxes were raised in Western Christendom to finance the Third Crusade, Saladin's brother al-'Adil would soon suggest an income tax of one per cent, centuries before such

Bitlis, with its formidable citadel, was on the frontier of the Artuqid and Zangid states, both of which eventually accepted Saladin's suzerainty. (Author's photograph)

The castle that the Templars built on the Bayt al-Ahzan overlooking the upper river Jordan at Jacob's Ford was not refortified after it fell to Saladin and so remains one of very few unmodified 12th-century Crusader castles. (Author's photograph)

an idea emerged in Europe. Even this would prove inadequate and so special taxes were imposed upon non-Muslims across Saladin's realm. Furthermore, the warfare initiated by Saladin's invasion in 1187, which only ended with the withdrawal of the Third Crusade in 1192, meant that the sultan's government purchased food and other commodities on a continuous and massive basis. As a result the price of foodstuffs rose steeply. For example in 1192 the cost of beans, the staple diet of Egypt, doubled.

In addition to economic and more-immediate military factors, there were broader diplomatic considerations. In the spring of 1187, while Saladin was still mobilizing his forces in Syria, a Byzantine imperial fleet raided Cyprus, which was held by Isaac Comnenus, a 'rebel' with strong links to the Crusader states. Although this attack stemmed from political rivalry inside the Byzantine Empire, it was widely viewed within the Crusader states as support for Saladin's looming attack.

Isma'ili 'Assassins' attempt to kill Saladin during his siege of Aleppo, 22 May 1175

On 22 May 1175, seven days after the start of his siege of Aleppo, Saladin was resting in the tent of one of his senior officers. With him was one of his guards, a Turkish mamluk whose name, Buzghush, meant 'grey falcon'. A group of warriors arrived and volunteered to join Saladin's guard. As they drew close to the tent, they were recognized by Nasih al-Din Khumartigin, lord of Bu Qubais and a close neighbour of the Isma'ili 'Assassin' mini-state in the hills of western Syria. When Nasih al-Din questioned the new arrivals they killed him and rushed towards the tent. At least one reached Saladin and struck his throat with a dagger. Fortunately the sultan was wearing a *kazaghand*, a cloth-covered and padded mail shirt. Saladin grasped the assassin's wrist and Buzghush grabbed the dagger blade, almost losing his fingers in the process. Another bodyguard then struck off the assassin's head while others cut down two more would-be killers outside.

Saladin himself certainly made full use of his improved relationship with the Byzantine ruling hierarchy in Constantinople. Meanwhile tensions between the Crusader states and the Byzantine Empire further undermined an already testy relationship between the Latin Catholic and Greek Orthodox Churches. Quite when close contact was made between Saladin and the Melkite Greek Orthodox hierarchy in Jerusalem is unclear, although the key man seems to have been Joseph, a Melkite Christian born in Jerusalem who now served as one of the sultan's aides. He would be credited with trying to get his fellow Melkites to open Jerusalem's gates following Saladin's great victory at the battle of Hattin. Perhaps this danger was known to the Crusader defenders and encouraged their decision to negotiate a quick surrender in 1187.

One of the most notable military successes of Saladin's reign was not on land, but at sea when Husam al-Din Lu'lu' wiped out the fleet sent into the Red Sea by Reynald of Châtillon in 1182–83. Egyptian shipwrights assembled prefabricated galleys here at Suez. (Author's photograph)

In this, the same year as the battle of Hattin, a Turcoman leader known to Armenians as Resdom raided the Cilician Kingdom of Armenia, which was a key ally of the Crusader states. In the event, Resdom was defeated and killed by King Leon of Armenia. Whether there was any connection between these raiders and Saladin is unknown, but the threat posed by such Turcoman tribes must have been on the mind of the ruler of the northernmost Crusader state, the Principality of Antioch, when he negotiated his own private truce with the sultan.

The invasion of the Kingdom of Jerusalem

The stages of the Hattin campaign were well recorded and are well known (see Campaign 19: *Hattin 1187*). It began when Saladin established a camp at the well-watered Ras al-Ma' south of Damascus on 13 March 1187. Here he summoned military contingents from across his realm while volunteers responded from even further afield. The fact that the Egyptian fleet began assembling at Alexandria indicated that this was going to be a major campaign. However, the process of mustering took many weeks and Saladin also had other duties, including leading a small contingent to Busra to protect the annual Hajj pilgrimage caravan. In April Saladin moved farther south, to yet again attack Reynald of Châtillon's castle of Karak.

Meanwhile, efforts were under way within the Crusader states to heal a rift between King Guy of Jerusalem and Count Raymond of Tripoli. On 30 April a delegation nominally led by Saladin's teenage son al-'Afdal sought permission from Count Raymond to cross his lands in Galilee, promising to cause no damage but heading for territory belonging to King Guy. Serious hostilities began the following day, 1 May, with a clash between a Muslim reconnaissance force under the experienced Turkish commander Muzaffar al-Din Gökböri and a relatively small Frankish contingent near the springs of Cresson. The Christians were badly mauled but Gökböri withdrew across the river Jordan that same day.

These were, however, mere preliminaries. Late in May, Saladin ordered his troops to muster at Tall 'Ashtarah, south of Ras al-Ma', while King Guy ordered his troops to muster near the Spring of Saffuriyah. It took almost a month for Saladin's men to assemble, with Taqi al-Din and the northern contingents amongst the last to arrive, having been delayed by the need to keep watch on the Principality of Antioch. On 26 June all seemed ready and the army's basic arrangement had been agreed. Taqi al-Din would command the right wing, Gökböri the left and Saladin the centre. The army was then reviewed before heading for Khisfin on the Golan Heights. Meanwhile King Guy was in council with his leading barons in Acre. The following day Saladin's army moved forward to al-Qahwani, next to the river Jordan and just inside the Kingdom of Jerusalem. Over the next few days the Christian troops completed their muster at Saffuriyah, where King Guy and the other barons joined them. Although there is disagreement about precisely when Saladin crossed the Jordan, it seems most likely that he did so on 30 June.

Tiberias was rapidly blockaded by some of Saladin's troops; other small units rode off to observe the enemy while the main force made camp as Kafr Sabt. There were a number of reliable water sources in the area between Tiberias and the Crusader camp at Saffuriyah, and on 1 July Saladin himself moved closer to the foe. He also conducted a detailed reconnaissance of the Lubia area. This lay on another route from Saffuriyah, which King Guy might choose to take if he wished to relieve Tiberias. On 2 July Saladin's infantry and engineers attacked Tiberias with siege engines. This was a risky strategy as it placed Saladin between enemies in Tiberias and Saffuriyah. Furthermore, Lake Tiberias now lay between Saladin's army and friendly territory across the Jordan. To guard against this danger the sultan remained at Kafr Sabt with most of his cavalry. By nightfall the town of Tiberias had fallen and its much-reduced garrison under Count Raymond's wife Eschiva withdrew to the citadel.

During the siege of Tiberias, King Guy and his advisors held an ill-tempered council at Saffuriyah where Count Raymond's cautious advice was overruled. Consequently the Christian army marched east on 3 July. They could chose between several roads because the old Roman road pattern, if not necessarily the roads themselves, was still in use. It is now clear that King Guy's troops followed these ancient routes wherever possible, but by holding Kafr Sabt, Saladin controlled the main route from Saffuriyah to

Qal'at al-Sudr, or Qal'at al-Gindi as it is more popularly known, was built for Saladin immediately before the 1187 campaign that culminated in his great victory at Hattin. Located on top of a bone-dry mountain in the Sinai desert, its water cisterns enabled the garrison to survive. (Author's photograph)

Conquest of Jerusalem and Third Crusade 1174–86 (frontiers c.1192)

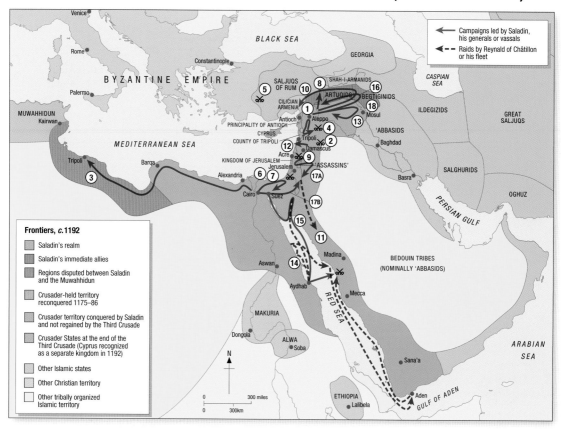

1. 1174–75: Saladin unsuccessfully besieges Nur al-Din's successor in Aleppo; Assassins attempt to kill Saladin; Crusader raid against Saladin's forces still besieging Citadel of Hims; Saladin abandons siege of Aleppo, instead completes siege of Hims and takes Baalbak (December 1174 to March 1175).

2. 1175: Saladin defeats Zangid counter-offensive by Aleppo and Mosul at Horns of Hama (13 April).

3. 1175: Saladin sends Qaraqush as part of continued competition with Muwahhidun to control Libya (summer).

4. 1176: Saladin defeats Zangids at Tall al-Sultan (22 April), then negotiates suzerainty over Aleppo (July).

5. 1176: Byzantine Emperor Manuel defeated by Saljuqs of Rum at Myriokephalon (17 September).

6. 1177: Sicilian-Norman fleet raids Tinnis (summer).

7. 1177: Raid by Saladin into Kingdom of Jerusalem is defeated at Tall al-Safiya (25 November).

8. 1178: Saladin defeats attempt by Saljuqs of Rum to besiege Raban (spring).

9. 1179: Saladin defeats Kingdom of Jerusalem at Marj al-'Uyun, takes the Templar castle at Bayt al-Ahzan (April–August).

10. 1180: Saladin intervenes in quarrel between Zangids of Mosul and Artuqids of Hisn Kayfa, convinces Saljuqs of Rum not to interfere, then raids Cilician Armenia.

11. 1181: Reynald of Châtillon raids the northern Hijaz (summer).

12. 1182: Saladin raids Kingdom of Jerusalem (July–August).

13. 1182: Saladin fails to take Zangid Mosul but captures Sinjar (December).

14. 1183: Reynald of Châtillon sends raiding fleet into the Red Sea (January–February), but penetration as far as Aden is unconfirmed.

15. 1183: Reynald of Châtillon's fleet is destroyed by Husam al-Din Lu'lu' near Rabigh (February).

16. 1183: Saladin takes Mayyafariqin, Mardin and Diyarbakir (May), imposes direct rule on Aleppo (June).

17. 1183: [A] Saladin raids the Kingdom of Jerusalem (September–October) then [B] summons an army from Egypt under al-'Adil for an unsuccessful joint attack on Karak (November–December).

18. 1186: Mosul recognizes Saladin's suzerainty (March).

19. 1187: Reynald of Châtillon breaks truce by capturing Muslim caravan, including members of Saladin's family (January or February).

20. 1187: Saladin establishes military camp at Ras al-Ma' and summons troops for jihad against Crusader states (March).

21. 1187: Taqi al-Din takes over the defence of the northern frontiers (March).

22. 1187: Saladin from Damascus and al-'Adil from Egypt join forces to raid Karak area (April).

23. 1187: Muslim reconnaissance force defeats Crusader force at springs of Cresson (1 May).

24. 1187: Saladin orders Ayyubid forces to muster at Tall 'Ashtarah (27 May).

Conquest of Jerusalem and Third Crusade 1187–93 (frontiers c.1192)

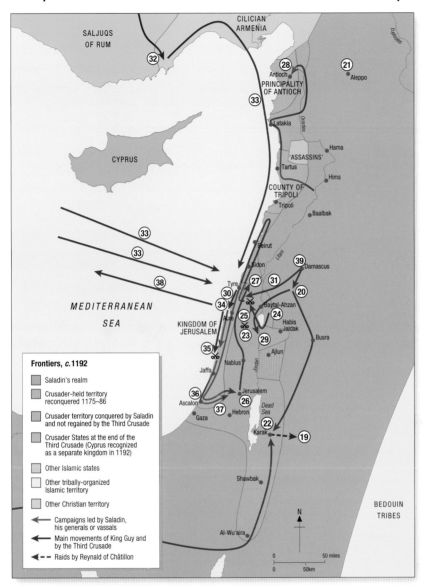

25 1187: Saladin invades Kingdom of Jerusalem, takes town but not Citadel of Tiberias (2 July), defeats Kingdom of Jerusalem and County of Tripoli at Hattin (4 July).

26 1187: Saladin retakes Acre (10 July), Sidon (29 July), Beirut (6 August), Ascalon (5 September) and Jerusalem (2 October).

27 1188: Saladin abandons siege of Tyre and disbands most of his army (1 January).

28 1188: Saladin takes Tartus town but not citadel, takes Latakia (22 July), and agrees truce with Principality of Antioch (26 September).

29 1188–89: Saladin takes castle of Belvoir (winter).

30 1189: King Guy of Jerusalem moves from Tyre to besiege Acre (28 August).

31 1189: Saladin moves against King Guy's siege (September).

32 1190: Emperor Frederick, leader of the German Imperial contingent of Third Crusade, drowns (10 June).

33 1189–91: Arrival of contingents of the Third Crusade at siege of Acre.

34 1191: Saladin's garrison in Acre surrenders (12 June); they and their families are massacred (20 August).

35 1191: Parallel marches by Saladin and forces of Third Crusade; attack by Saladin is defeated at Arsuf (7 September).

36 1191: Saladin demolishes fortifications of Ascalon (10–11 September), pulls back to Ramla and then Latrun, disbands most of his army, falls back to Jerusalem (12 December).

37 1192: Skirmishing between forces of Saladin and Third Crusade (January–August), peace agreement signed between representatives of Saladin and King Richard (2 September).

38 1192: King Richard sails homeward from Acre (October).

39 1193: Saladin dies in Damascus (3 March).

Tiberias. Hence King Guy's often-criticized decision to take a more northerly road was in fact tactically sensible. Furthermore, the Israeli historian Benjamin Kedar has shown that most of the Crusaders' supposed blunders were nothing of the kind and although they failed to reach the springs of Hattin they probably had a realistic chance of doing so.

Saladin appears to have been outside Tiberias when news of the enemy's move reached him. He left a small force to watch the citadel and promptly led his guard regiment back to his main camp at Kafr Sabt. Small forces were soon harassing the Crusaders' line of march but Saladin and the main force only made contact with King Guy's army when the Christians reached Tur'an around mid-morning. Here there was a small spring where a few men from the Christians' left flank were probably able to drink.

The carving above the main gate of Saladin's castle of Qal'at al-Sudr used the same shield-and-sword motif used almost a century earlier on one of the ceremonial gates of the Fatimid Caliphate's fortified palace-city of Cairo. (Author's photograph)

This copper dirham, minted at Mayyafariqin in 587 AH [1190/01 AD] shows Saladin wearing the *sharbush* hat of a Saljuq-style Turkish ruler. (University Library, inv. no. 2009/0547, Leipzig)

Hattin – the decisive victory

From this point on Saladin's attempts to encircle the enemy became gradually more effective, and he also sent troops to control the springs of Hattin, where the Christians might be heading. On the other side the increasingly thirsty, hot and dusty Christian army faced frequent long-distance harassment by archery. This was a significant threat to their animals, including the knights' horses, though less so to the men. The road from Tur'an to Tiberias divided a short distance west of Lubia, at a place known to the Crusaders as Marescalia, now identified either as the hamlet of Khirbat Maskana lying close to the Roman road, or as the man-made pool of Birkat Maskana between the road and Khirbat Maskana. This could hold water even in July if properly maintained, as was probably the case in 1187. The vanguard of the Christian army under Count Raymond stopped at Maskana because the line of march behind them was being slowed down and dangerously extended by enemy harassment.

At this point there was probably a change in the Christian plan. Believing that the army could not fight its way through or across the front of Saladin's main army in the hills south of the road, Raymond persuaded Guy to veer to the left and head for the springs of Hattin. From here they could march down to Tiberias the following day. The village of Hattin was believed to be the site of the grave of Shu'ayb, the Biblical Prophet Jethro, while the neighbouring hills known as the Horns of Hattin were regarded by some eastern Christians as the site of Christ's Sermon on the Mount. Of more immediate relevance to the forthcoming battle, the ancient Bronze Age walls around the Horns of Hattin were probably taller in the 12th century than they are today. Together

Arab Bedouin grazing their flocks on spring grass in the Syrian desert south of the river Euphrates. Although Arab soldiers were severely downgraded in Saladin's new military system, large numbers were still recruited for special purposes, most notably as high-speed raiding forces and as ambush troops. (Author's photograph)

with walled field systems south and south-east of the Horns, they would have provided the infantry of both sides with protection against opposing cavalry.

At this point the Christian army was probably spread over some 2km in a relatively flat and broad valley. The Jabal Tur'an hills stretched along the northern flank, ending with a small hill topped by the village of Nimrin. Beyond a narrow gorge that led down to the village of Hattin and its spring rose the low volcanic peaks of the Horns of Hattin. Beyond them the ground fell steeply towards Lake Tiberias. Not far from the Christian army's right or southern flank rose other wooded hills, amidst which nestled the villages of Shajara and Lubia. Just visible down the valley was the welcoming blue of Lake Tiberias, 12km away but perhaps seeming closer to the thirsty Crusader army.

Most sources agree that the Christian army's change of direction led to considerable confusion. Saladin, who had a clear view from the southern hills, recognized what the enemy were trying to do, so he sent Taqi al-Din's division to block their path. The fact that he was able to do so is further evidence of the superior speed and manoeuvrability of the Muslim forces. Saladin now established his field headquarters at Lubia for the night. Gökböri, in command of Saladin's left wing, was almost certainly in the hills around Shajara and it was probably his troops whose earlier attacks had forced the enemy's rearguard to a halt, thus slowing the Christians down and convincing their leaders to veer north towards a closer source of drinking water. Charges by the Crusader knights failed to drive them away and it was around this time that Count Raymond reportedly cried out: 'Alas! Alas! Lord God, the war is over. We are betrayed to death and the land is lost!'

Now the Christian army made camp near Maskana. Presumably Guy and Raymond hoped that, rested and reorganized, their men could make a dash for the Spring of Hattin the following morning. In fact the tired and thirsty Christians spent the night listening to the Muslims playing drums, singing and praying – evidence of the Muslims' increasing confidence. The fact that the night before the battle of Hattin was also the 'Night of Khidr', a time of religious celebration for Muslims, must also have played a part. Saladin meanwhile brought up the rest of his army from Kafr Sabt, probably including infantry,

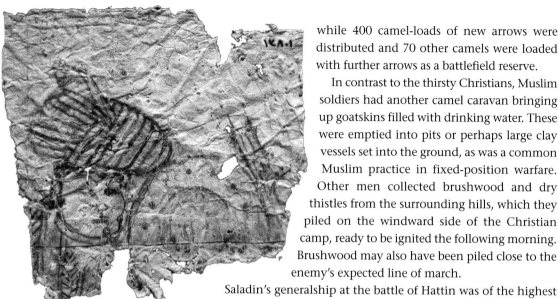

while 400 camel-loads of new arrows were distributed and 70 other camels were loaded with further arrows as a battlefield reserve.

In contrast to the thirsty Christians, Muslim soldiers had another camel caravan bringing up goatskins filled with drinking water. These were emptied into pits or perhaps large clay vessels set into the ground, as was a common Muslim practice in fixed-position warfare. Other men collected brushwood and dry thistles from the surrounding hills, which they piled on the windward side of the Christian camp, ready to be ignited the following morning. Brushwood may also have been piled close to the enemy's expected line of march.

Saladin's generalship at the battle of Hattin was of the highest order, which did not mean that the Crusader leadership was necessarily poor. It might be more correct to suggest that the Crusader army was outfought rather than outgeneralled. Saladin's success resulted from getting his army into battle in a location and under circumstances where it was able to make full use of its strengths while minimizing its weaknesses. On the other side the army of the Crusader Kingdom of Jerusalem and its allies in the County of Tripoli were forced to fight where the Westerners' strengths – most notably charges by close-packed *conrois* units of heavily armoured cavalry – were minimized. It has been suggested that Saladin's tactics were highly risky, though in several respects they were straight out of books on military arts that had been written in the Islamic world since the 8th century.

This damaged drawing of a turbaned soldier with a round shield, plus two javelins held by a soldier next to him, was found in the abandoned ruins of Fustat in southern Cairo. It dates from the 12th century or perhaps a little earlier. (Museum of Islamic Art, Ms. 13801, Cairo; author's photograph)

Thereafter the course of the battle was relatively straightforward. The three divisions of the Christian army re-formed into squares or rectangles, with cavalry and baggage in the centre surrounded and protected by infantry. Saladin did not interfere with these preparations, perhaps unsure whether his enemies intended to fight their way to the springs or to attack his own position in the hills

Quite when the brushfires were lighted is unclear, but according to the anonymous *Continuation of the History of William of Tyre*:

> Early next morning Saladin ordered that they should light the fires in the barriers which he had had made all round the Christians. They soon did this, and the fires burned vigorously and the smoke from the fires was great; and this, together with the heat of the sun above them caused them discomfort and great harm... When the fires were lit and the smoke was great, the Saracens surrounded the host and shot their darts through the smoke and so wounded and killed men and horses.

This may have been before the Christians started to move, or during their initial march towards Hattin, or during the collapse of cohesion on the plateau beneath the Horns. Or it may have been a continuous process throughout much of the day's fighting. Given Saladin's careful preparations, the latter seems likely, with fires being lit in sequence by volunteers including Saladin's numerous *muttawiya* auxiliaries.

At some point early in the day one or more knights with experience of fighting as mercenaries in Muslim armies urged King Guy to attack Saladin's position vigorously. They were overruled and the Christian army either started or continued its painful march towards the Spring of Hattin, some 5km away. The Christians' morale was now declining and around this time six knights and some sergeants deserted to Saladin, urging him to close in for the kill as their comrades were as good as beaten. Might these men, rather than being the villains described by the chroniclers, actually have been heroes attempting to make Saladin launch a premature assault?

Saladin apparently now sent his centre and perhaps his left flank under Gökböri into the attack. The Templars counter-charged while Raymond of Tripoli's vanguard also charged, probably against Taqi al-Din and the Muslim right wing. The only chronicler to hint at how close the enemy came to breaking through is Ibn Khallikan in his biographies of Taqi al-Din and Gökböri, who wrote: 'They both held their ground although the whole army was routed and driven back. The soldiers then heard that these two chiefs still resisted the enemy, whereupon they returned to the charge and victory was decided in favour of the Muslims.'

Of course it was less straightforward than that. The Crusader knights drove back the Muslim cavalry but lost many of their own horses. More significantly, the morale of the hard-pressed, smoke-blinded and desperately thirsty Christian infantry began to crack, with ever-larger numbers drifting eastwards.

Above: Although Turks and Kurds dominated Saladin's armies, Arabs still played a significant role. The men shown in this copy of the *maqamat* by al-Hariri are preparing to escort a caravan from Damascus to Baghdad. (Institute of Oriental Studies, C-23, f.109, St Petersburg, via V. A. Livskity)

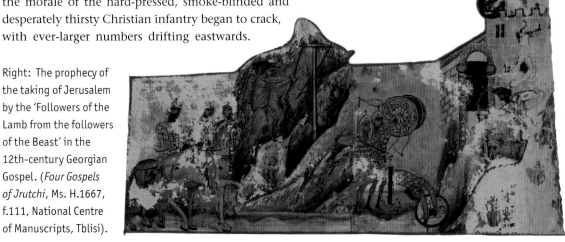

Right: The prophecy of the taking of Jerusalem by the 'Followers of the Lamb from the followers of the Beast' in the 12th-century Georgian Gospel. (*Four Gospels of Jrutchi*, Ms. H.1667, f.111, National Centre of Manuscripts, Tblisi).

This simple but highly decorated steel helmet probably dates from the 13th century. Its light weight and simple shape is in stark contrast to the increasingly heavy and cumbersome armours favoured by the Crusaders. (Furusiyya Art Foundation, London)

They are unlikely to have been hoping to reach Lake Tiberias, as sometimes suggested, but probably sought refuge within the Bronze Age walls on the Horns of Hattin. Nevertheless, these movements would seem to have taken the exhausted foot soldiers through the middle of Saladin's army, which clearly cannot have been the case. A possible explanation may be found in the fact that Taqi al-Din blocked the road to Hattin by holding a position from the foot of the Horns to the hill of Nimrin, thus opening up a gap between his men and Saladin's centre.

King Guy now ordered his fragmenting army to halt and erect tents around which the men could assemble, but in the confusion only three were put up – probably a short distance west or south-west of the Horns of Hattin. Smoke from the brushfires may still have been burning, and at that time of year the prevailing wind was from the west, so any Muslim troops beneath the Horns would have suffered as much as their enemies. About this time the Count of Tripoli made what became his notorious charge northwards and escaped the forthcoming debacle. Yet this was not an act of treachery, being instead an attempt to break the Muslim encirclement and enable the Christian army to reach the springs of Hattin.

Rather than trying to stop Raymond's heavy cavalry, Taqi al-Din's nimble horsemen and perhaps infantry swung aside and let the Christian knights continue into the gorge leading to Hattin village. It was not their impetus that made it impossible for the Christians to return, but the lie of the land and the fact that the Muslims closed up behind them. In reality Raymond had almost no alternative other than to continue down the Wadi Hammam towards Lake Tiberias. There, instead of joining his wife in the trap that was the Citadel of Tiberias, he headed north to the coastal city of Tyre.

Back on the plateau the rest of the Christian army was falling into ever-greater confusion as most of the infantry streamed towards the apparent security of the northern Horn of Hattin. Perhaps they had been hoping to follow Raymond northwards to support his charge, or they may have been looking for an escape route. Once the path to Hattin village was closed again it would seem natural for them to establish a defensive position on the closer (though lower) northern Horn. Morale now collapsed, with the infantry on the Horn refusing to come down again to rejoin what remained of the Christian cavalry around the three erected tents. Meanwhile Muslim archers shot down the knights' almost unprotected horses until most of the Crusader cavalry were also fighting on foot.

There was nothing for King Guy to do but order his entire army onto the Horns. Here the knights are said to have established a position on the taller but flat-topped southern Horn where the bright red royal tent was also erected. Quite when the Muslims captured the Christians' most sacred relic, the Holy Cross, is unclear, though it is known to have been taken by Taqi al-Din's division. Its loss would have had a devastating impact upon Christian morale, whereupon the Muslims attacked the Horns of Hattin from all sides. The northern and eastern slopes were too steep for cavalry, so Muslim foot soldiers scrambled up to attack enemy infantry on the northern Horn from the rear. By mid-afternoon this northern Horn had been taken, so Saladin ordered Taqi al-Din to charge the Christian knights and others who were making a final stand on the southern Horn.

The southern slope of the southern Horn is also steep, though not impossible for cavalry. It would seem that Saladin himself was now watching this sector, so perhaps Taqi al-Din led his men up the gentler western slope, which led to the saddle between the Horns. The Christians were not beaten yet, and the knights made a number of counter-charges, one of which came close to Saladin. Perhaps the Crusaders hoped to kill the sultan and thus save the day. Twice the Muslim cavalry surged up the slope until they won the saddle between the Horns. Eventually the red royal tent fell, marking the end of the battle of Hattin. It had been a brutal struggle with significant losses on both sides. Nevertheless, those who suffered most were the Christian infantry and the knights' horses. While large numbers of knights sank to the ground in utter exhaustion to be captured, Muslim accounts note that very few enemy horses were taken.

Eight carved figures survive on this late 12th- or early 13th-century throne niche from al-Han, an area under Saladin's suzerainty in the Sinjar hills west of Mosul. (Iraqi National Museum, Baghdad, author's photograph)

Taking advantage of success

Saladin wasted no time in letting everyone know about his victory, not least the 'Abbasid caliph in Baghdad. His letter to the caliph summed it up with the words:

> The King was captured, and this was a hard day for the unbelievers. The Prince [Reynald of Châtillon], may God curse him, was taken and the servant [Saladin himself] harvested his seed, killing him with his own hand and so fulfilling his vow. A number of the leaders of his state and the great men of his false religion were taken prisoner, while the dead numbered more than forty thousand. Not one of the Templars survived. It was a day of grace, on which the wolf and the vulture kept company, while death and captivity followed in turns. The unbelievers were tied together in fetters, astride chains rather than stout horses.[4]

4 Melville, C. P. and Lyons, M. C., 'Saladin's Hattin Letter' in Kedar, B. Z. (ed.), *The Horns of Hattin*, (Variorum: London & Jerusalem, 1992) p. 212.

While his troops were flushed with victory, Saladin used the momentum of his campaign to retake as much of the Crusader states as possible before winter came and campaigning had to end. In this he was assisted by the fact that most of the Kingdom of Jerusalem's fighting men had been with King Guy's army at the battle of Hattin. Many were dead or captured or scattered. Few got home in time to significantly help defend the castles, fortified towns and cities

The two summits of the Horns of Hattin do not look as dramatic from the west as they do from the east. Yet it was here that the 'Franks', as the Western European Christians were known to the Muslims, made their final stand. (Author's photograph)

of the Kingdom. In many cases the fate of such places was not even recorded. They simply fell and are next mentioned in written sources as containing Muslim garrisons. Saladin's task was also made easier by the fact that in many places the local Muslim and Jewish populations rose up against the Crusaders. In the Nablus area, for example, rebels forced the remaining Franks into their castles before Saladin's troops arrived.

In addition to seizing often almost undefended fortifications, the Muslims found abundant booty. According to one Latin source, the anonymous author of *De Expugnatione Terrae Sanctae per Saladinum* who himself witnessed many of these events, al-'Adil captured large quantities of military equipment at Jaffa. Not surprisingly Muslim morale was sky-high as Saladin's army marched towards Jerusalem. Ahead of the main army, units of Turcoman and

Saladin and his son al-'Afdal at the battle of Hattin, 4 July 1187

Having been almost surrounded on the flat land west of the twin-peaked hill known as the Horns of Hattin, King Guy of Jerusalem followed his demoralized infantry up onto the hill. Whereas the foot soldiers gathered on the northern Horn, the knights established a position on the flat-topped southern Horn, where King Guy's royal tent was probably erected as a rallying point. By mid-afternoon the northern Horn had been taken by Saladin's troops, but the Christians were not yet beaten and the knights made a number of counter-charges. Saladin's 17-year-old son al-'Afdal, for whom this was his first experience of real battle, later described these events to the chronicler Ibn al-'Athir: 'When I saw that the Franks withdrew, pursued by the Muslims, I shouted for joy: "We have beaten them!" But the Franks rallied and charged again and drove the Muslims back to my father. He acted as he had on the first occasion and the Muslims turned upon the Franks and drove them back to the hill. Again I shouted "We have beaten them!" but my father rounded on me and said "Be quiet! We have not beaten them until that tent falls." As he was speaking to me the tent fell. The sultan dismounted, prostrated himself in thanks to God Almighty and wept for joy.'[5]

5   Ibn al-Athir (tr. Richards, D. S.), *The Chronicle of Ibn al-Athir for the Crusading Period, part 2: The Age of Nur al-Din and Saladin* (Aldershot, 2007) p. 323.

Bedouin tribal auxiliaries ranged far and wide, capturing 'Frankish' families at Mount Carmel, Sidon, Jaffa, Lydda, Ramla and elsewhere.

Presumably in expectation of a bitterly contested siege, Saladin's siege engineers sent men to cut down olive and other branches to make *zaribas*. These were not siege engines but screens to defend archers, engineers, miners or other men within archery range of the defenders. There also seems to have been some confusion about the strength of Jerusalem's fortifications in 1187. It now appears that there was no real citadel in the city. Instead the Tower of David essentially consisted of the Herodian Tower, which had served as Jerusalem's strongest defensive structure since Roman times. In the event there was little fighting, and Saladin quickly negotiated a surrender. Furthermore, it was not until 1191, with a looming threat from the Third Crusade, that Saladin even had the city's walls repaired. A new moat was then excavated while the towers between the Damascus and Jaffa Gates were renovated. Even then there was no mention of a citadel, the first probably being erected by the Crusaders during their short-lived second occupation of the city in 1229–39. If there had been an early Islamic, Umayyad-period fortress attached to the ancient Herodian Tower of David as some archaeologists suggest, it would seem to have fallen out of use by the 12th century.

For the rest of 1187 Saladin and his army concentrated on recapturing as much territory of the Crusader states as they could. Following the established strategic traditions of the medieval Islamic world, Saladin mopped up the easiest targets first and avoided confrontations which would have slowed the momentum of his campaign. In so doing he maintained both the morale of his troops and his own prestige. Both were of supreme importance, especially for a relatively new ruler whose position remained vulnerable to charges of usurpation.

Not surprisingly, Saladin sought friends and allies where he could. In Lebanon he unexpectedly found them amongst the staunchly Shia Druze who, because of their own tenuous position as a new community that was widely regarded as heretical, were equally keen to find a powerful ally. The Druze leader currently holding the stronghold of Sarahmul was Jamal al-Din Hajji, whose father Karama had been ally of Nur al-Din. Hajji was the youngest of four brothers who, at the age of seven, had been hidden by his widowed mother when his three elder brothers were assassinated by Crusaders from Beirut. The latter also devastated Sarahmul. In 1187 Hajji was 20 years old and burning for revenge, so when Saladin came to attack Beirut he went to meet the sultan at Khaldeh. After the surrender of Beirut, according to the Druze chronicler Salih Ibn Yahya, Saladin touched Hajji's head and said: 'There, we have avenged you from the Franks, be of good cheer, you shall continue in the place of your father and your brothers.' Saladin thereupon issued a

The letter in Latin that Saladin sent to the German Emperor Frederick I Barbarossa in 1188 announcing his victory over the Crusader Kingdom of Jerusalem. (Staatsbibliothek Berlin-Preussischer Kulturbesitz, Ms. Theol. Lat. Quart. 190, f.77r, Berlin)

manshur, or official certificate, confirming the villages that would form Hajji's *'iqta* or fief.

The coincidence of Conrad of Monferrat's arrival on the coast of Lebanon, where he supplied military assistance to Reynald of Sidon in Tyre, caught Saladin by surprise. Conrad had in fact started his journey to the Holy Land before Saladin's campaign began. Surrender negotiations were actually under way between Reynald of Sidon and Saladin when Conrad suddenly appeared. These were now broken off and Saladin decided against pursuing a slow siege with no guarantee of success. Instead he disbanded half his army. The men were tired but triumphant, perhaps laden with booty and certainly eager to go home. Later military historians have generally regarded this as a catastrophic decision, but in reality Saladin was acting in accordance with the established Islamic strategy of his day. Indeed, the sultan was still outside Tyre when he received a congratulatory embassy from the Byzantine Emperor Isaac Angelus, Saladin

having previously sent news of his victories to Constantinople. In return the Byzantine ambassadors gave him military equipment that their Emperor had taken from recently defeated Sicilian-Norman invaders in Greece.

After liberating the holy city of Jerusalem, Saladin took his forces northwards to retake considerable Crusader territory in north-west Syria, including the city of Tartus and the outer part of its citadel. (Author's photograph)

Once Saladin's troops had rested, some contingents were recalled in the spring of 1188. What followed was an interesting and daring campaign, which sheds considerable light on Saladin's strategic priorities. It was analysed in a thesis by John Winthrop Hackett, who later became one of Britain's most successful officers during World War II.[6] He quoted the chronicler 'Imad al-Din, who said of Antioch that to take away her fortress was to take away her life. In his study Hackett paid particular attention to the road system in north-western Syria, which was dominated by several north–south links but very few running east to west. This presented Saladin with significant problems because his own centres of strength remained the inland cities lying east of the coastal mountains, whereas the strength of the northern Crusader states rested upon coastal cities that could, of course, be resupplied by sea.

Campaigning along the coastal strip meant that mountains lay between Saladin and the inland cities. On this occasion his daring strategy meant that he could ill afford to leave behind any fortifications that a newly arrived Crusader army might use. Hence he spent eight days supervising the destruction of the city walls and the captured outer part of the Citadel of Tartus to make it indefensible without major reconstruction. Saladin also wanted to await the arrival of a large force of specialist siege troops from Aleppo before extending his campaign into even more dangerous territory. The varied nature of the problems Saladin had to overcome was highlighted by the fact that

---

6   Hackett, J. W., *Saladin's Campaign of 1188 in Northern Syria*, MS.B.Litt thesis, University of Oxford, 1937.

The soldier on this 12th-century Egyptian lustre-ware bowl is certainly an infantryman and carries the elongated shield first developed for use on foot. (V & A Museum study collection, London, author's photograph)

Crusader galleys could come so close to the shore that their archers shot at Muslim troops as they marched along one stretch of coastal road. Furthermore the neighbouring hills were so steep and inaccessible that Saladin's army could not move inland. The only answer was for Saladin's pioneers to erect a temporary breastwork along the seaward side of road, manned by archers who shot back at the enemy's ships.

This campaign involved a number of sieges, one of the most interesting being that of the Crusader castle of Sahyun in July 1188. By walking the ground and using a trained military eye, Hackett identified dead ground to the south-east of one of the main towers, where troops could have assembled in relative safety before launching their assault. The chronicler 'Imad al-Din did in fact mention 'an angle of the ditch which the Franks had neglected to fortify' at Sahyun. On the other hand Muslim chroniclers often exaggerated the steepness of the approach to these Crusader castles in order to accentuate the wonder of their eventual conquest.

Sahyun finally fell on 29 July 1188. Saladin then established his camp on high ground just west of the castle of Hisn Barziya, known to the Crusaders as Bourzay, on 21 August. A bombardment failed because the lie of the land gave a clear advantage to the defenders' stone-throwing mangonels, so Saladin decided to use his numerical superiority to wear down the enemy and take advantage of the length of Barziya's walls. This resulted in a sequence of relatively small attacks in different places throughout the heat of the day. Eventually the victory shouts of Muslim prisoners held within the castle's keep made the exhausted Christian defenders think the enemy had broken in, so they surrendered. This unusual siege can be seen as a clear example of successful psychological warfare.

There were further and sometimes quite hard-fought sieges before Saladin's army arrived before the walls of the massive black stone fortress of Baghras on 17 September. Here he followed the procedure outlined in classic Islamic military manuals of the day, sending forward lightly armed troops to invest the place before his main army arrived. Nine days of siege were then sufficient to convince the defenders to surrender, but instead of going on to attack Antioch and thus wipe out the eponymous Principality, Saladin agreed a truce. This was a disappointment to many in the Islamic Middle East, though it reflected the fact that Saladin's army and probably also his treasury were almost exhausted. Discipline had been declining for weeks and the professional soldiers wanted to go home to their families and to attend to their 'iqta fiefs. The volunteers similarly wanted to get back to their farms or businesses. Saladin's authority clearly had limits, as would be made brutally clear in subsequent years.

The limitations of victory

The strategic situation grew more difficult for Saladin during the course of 1189, although things at first looked like they would continue as before. In early May news came of the taking of Shawbak in Oultrejordain, which meant that Saladin had reconquered the entire Crusader Kingdom of Jerusalm except for the port city of Tyre and one nearby castle – Shaqif Arnun. In the north he had regained the entire Principality of Antioch except for Antioch and the castle of al-Qusair. In contrast, the County of Tripoli had lost little territory, so this was where Saladin now decided to focus his attention. In the event, the intended campaign did not take place because Saladin could not resist the apparent opportunity of retaking Reynald of Sidon's strategic castle of Shaqif Arnun, known to the Crusaders as Beaufort.

Reynald of Sidon had escaped the debacle of Hattin. He now used his fluency in Arabic and knowledge of Islam to build a relationship of trust with Saladin. However, this episode also illustrates a certain naivety in Saladin, as hinted at by the later Arabic chronicler al-'Umari:

> His knowledge of Arabic literature and his interest in Islam made Saladin listen to him. Reynald even hinted that he might settle as a convert in Damascus. He said that he was willing to surrender his castle but he wanted three months to settle his affairs. When this period had passed Reynald was taken under escort to the castle where he ordered the garrison-commander in Arabic to surrender and in French to resist. The Arabs were not taken in, and Reynald was cast into prison in Damascus. Saladin let his amirs continue the siege summer and winter and after a year the fortress capitulated. Saladin forgave Reynald his trickery and released him.[7]

This tiny bronze figure of a horseman comes from Iran and dates from the 12th or early 13th century. (Museum of Islamic Art, Cairo, author's photograph)

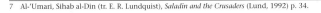

7   Al-'Umari, Sihab al-Din (tr. E. R. Lundquist), *Saladin and the Crusaders* (Lund, 1992) p. 34.

Stone ammunition to be shot from a mangonel, found in Saladin's castle outside Ajlun. The larger missile could only have been shot from the sort of massive counterweight mangonel used in the 13th century, but the smaller ones might even date from Saladin's reign. (Castle Museum, Ajlun; author's photograph)

The year 1188 had seen several powerful Western European monarchs 'take the cross' and promise to lead a massive new Crusade to reconquer the Holy Land (see Campaign 161: *The Third Crusade 1191*). Saladin would soon have been aware of this, and of the fact that the first contingent of this Third Crusade set out under the command of Emperor Frederick of Germany in May 1189. During the first weeks of June that year troops from the city of Tyre, the last remaining fragment of the Kingdom of Jerusalem, tried to retake Sidon but failed. However the early summer also saw the arrival of a fleet from the warlike Italian merchant republic of Pisa to support the Crusader enclave at Tyre.

Saladin was not a man to sit back and await events. Although he was not in a position to launch a full-scale siege of Tyre, his troops were involved in skirmishes, something that illustrates both the tactics and the tactical limitations of Saladin's army. Then King Guy suddenly led his small force from Tyre to besiege the garrison that Saladin had installed in Acre. It was the start of one of the longest and most epic sieges in the history of the Crusades. This extraordinary campaign became even more complicated when Saladin moved against Guy, besieging the besiegers, on 15 September, and this double siege only ended when Acre fell to the forces of the Third Crusade on 12 July 1191. There was of course considerable open battle as well as fixed-position 'trench warfare' during this siege. One of the first major clashes took place in September 1189 when a Christian force advanced and was attacked by fully armoured Muslim 'heavy cavalry', culminating in hand-to-hand combat with swords.

A more serious clash on 4 October was described by al-'Umari, who noted how close the fighting came to Saladin himself. On the other hand, al-'Umari's claim that victory went to the Muslims was misleading:

> The Franks had gathered and they attacked the sultan's centre and drove the soldiers from their position. They kept killing the Muslims until they reached the sultan's tent. But the sultan and his attendants had withdrawn and stayed aside. The support of the Franks was cut off while they were engaged in the fight against the sultan's right wing... The sultan attacked the Franks who were breaking through his right wing and directed his troops against them. The Franks were destroyed and fell in the battle. Nearly three thousand Franks were killed this time. Some of the Muslims fled to Tiberias, some of them reached Damascus.

Al-'Umari then described how the stench of decaying corpses led to sickness that infected Saladin himself. Consequently the Muslim camp was moved to al-Kharruba on Mount Carmel on 26 October 1189, which in turn enabled the Crusaders to press their siege of Acre more closely.

Saladin's previous belligerent behaviour towards neighbouring Muslim rulers meant that little help was

Scholars still argue about the real function of the many small but thick-walled earthenware 'grenades' found in and around castles and fortifications of the medieval Islamic world. (Ajlun Castle Museum; author's photograph)

forthcoming, while his naval weakness meant that Crusader reinforcements poured into the besiegers' camp by sea. Perhaps more in hope than expectation he sent a letter to Abu Yusuf Ya'qub al-Mansur, the Muwahhid ruler of North Africa and Islamic Spain, seeking his support, especially as the Muwahhidun had a powerful and effective fleet: 'How could he see the lands of Kufr [Unbelief] aiding Kufr in the Holy Land, while the lands of Islam, failing to support Islam … let him [the Muwahhid ruler al-Mansur] fill the sea with sailing ships, carrying for the Muslims [in the East] war supplies, men, or any form of help… Let him help the People of the Faith against the People of Misfortune [the Franks].' In January 1190 Saladin received a reply, refusing to help.

Later that year Saladin supposedly received another letter, this time from his unofficial ally the Byzantine Emperor, informing him that prayers were being said in his name in the mosque in Constantinople, and also to apologize for allowing the massive German contingent of the Third Crusade to pass through Byzantine territory. By this stage Saladin was in need of more than warm words. Throughout 1190 the brutal double siege of Acre continued, and according to Saladin's friend and biographer Baha al-Din the sultan used every trick he knew to try and weaken the Crusaders' ever-tightening grip around the city: 'When the enemy moved, aiming for the head of the river, he circled around behind them to cut them off from their tents, riding for a while and then dismounting to rest, shading himself with a kerchief on his head from the severe effect of the sun but not erecting a tent for himself so that the enemy would not spy any weakness.' On another occasion on 23 November 1190 Saladin's troops ambushed a large body of heavily armoured Crusader cavalry and seem to have hit the enemy in the flank, unhorsing many knights. This sounds like a particularly successful application of a manoeuvre described in detail in several early medieval *furusiyya* manuals.

By 1191, with the siege and counter-siege of Acre dragging on, Saladin had to use all his leadership skills to maintain the flagging morale of his tired troops. Once again Baha al-Din provides detailed descriptions of a leader he clearly admired:

> Every day, when the sultan was in close contact with them [the Crusaders at the siege of Acre] he had to make a circuit around the enemy once or twice. When the battle was fierce, he would ride between the two battle lines, accompanied by a page leading a spare mount, and cross between the armies from right to left, disposing the battalions and ordering them to advance or halt in positions that he thought fit, all the time observing the enemy at close quarters.

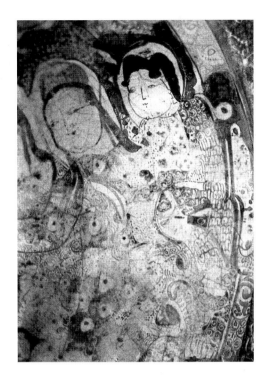

A guardsman in a long lamellar cuirass appears on this lustre-ware bowl made in Iran or Egypt in the 12th or early 13th century, squeezed against the edge, behind the main subjects. (Museum of Islamic Art, inv. no. 13279, Cairo; author's photograph)

Tibnin, 24 July 1189

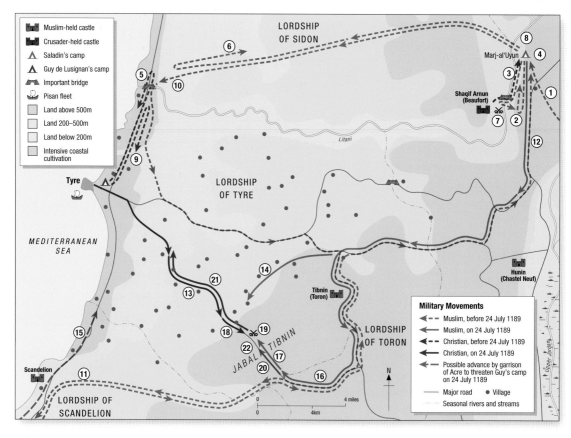

Guy of Lusignan, the captured King of Jerusalem, was released by Saladin during the summer of 1188. He swore not to fight against the Muslims but soon broke this oath. After Conrad of Monferrat refused to hand over Tyre, Guy took refuge in Tripoli where 200 knights from Sicily arrived and saved the city from Saladin. In April 1189 Guy returned to Tyre but Conrad still refused to hand it over, so Guy and his army made camp outside its fortifications. The arrival of a fleet of 52 ships from the Italian maritime republic of Pisa, commanded by Archbishop Ubaldo, arrived on 6 April, marking the military beginning of the Third Crusade. Soon afterwards Ubaldo quarrelled with Conrad and offered his support to Guy, who similarly won the support of Sicilian troops from Tripoli. Meanwhile the Crusader Kingdom still held the powerful castle of Shaqif Arnun (Beaufort), which guarded the upper end of the Litani river gorge. Other castles in this region, including Tibnin (Toron), were now held by Saladin's garrisons.

Events

1 Saladin leaves Damascus (21 April) to attack Shaqif Arnun, marching via Marj al-Barghuth near Banyas, where the various elements of his forces reassembled, before establishing his camp on the fertile meadows of Marj al-'Uyun (5 May).

2 Further units join Saladin's camp, while the sultan studies the castle every day.

3 Reynald of Sidon, lord of Shaqif Arnun, goes to Saladin's camp to negotiate and hints that he might convert to Islam. He is also credited with shouting to his garrison to surrender in Arabic but to resist in French.

4 Saladin receives a letter from al-Qadi al-Fadil informing him of the birth of his grandson (17 June).

5 Frankish troops cross the Litani bridge dividing the lordships of Tyre and Sidon.

6 Saladin gathers a force (3 July) and hurries to the scene but finds the enemy already repulsed.

7 Saladin makes his daily reconnaissance of Shaqif Arnun (5 July) but is joined by a crowd of what were described as 'volunteers, common folk and Bedouin' who think he intends an assault. Refusing to disperse, they cross the bridge and are struck by a Frankish cavalry charge, and many are killed.

8 Because of the disaster on 5 July, Saladin decides on an offensive.

9 King Guy marches towards the Litani crossing and makes camp, but then retreats.

10 Saladin moves out of Marj al-'Uyun (13 July) but his advance guard informs him that the enemy has again retreated. Land communications between Crusader-held Tyre and Tripoli are now definitively cut.

11 Saladin decides that Guy it likely to attack Tibnin or Acre, so he inspects their defences.

12 Saladin returns to Marj 'Uyun (22 July) to await the end of the truce that he has agreed with Reynald of Sidon. Saladin also learns that enemy foragers are ranging as far as Jabal Tibnin to collect fuel, so he decides to ambush them.

13 Frankish foragers and their cavalry escort, reportedly commanded by King Guy, leave camp outside Tyre.

14 Saladin's garrison in Tibnin is ordered to emerge with a small force to harass the enemy foragers on the morning of 24 July, but to flee back to Tibnin if pursued by enemy cavalry.

15 Saladin's garrison in Acre is ordered to threaten the main Frankish camp if the main enemy army moves to support its foragers, but there is no evidence that it did so.

16 Saladin and his main force leave camp at dawn (24 July) and reach a spot close to the place where the Tibnin garrison will harass the Frankish foragers.

17 Saladin divides his force into eight divisions, from each of which he selects 20 of those regarded as the bravest men on the best horses. The latter are instructed to make themselves look like a badly hidden ambush in order to draw the enemy into combat, and then to retreat, pulling their pursuers towards Saladin's real ambush.

18 King Guy learns of the threatened ambush and draws his cavalry into battle formation.

19 A fight develops between the Franks and the false ambush, and according to Baha al-Din the latter are 'too proud to retreat and induced by their zeal to disobey the sultan and to meet a numerous enemy with such a little band'. The struggle continues until late in the day but the false ambush did not, or could not, warn Saladin of the delay in their planned retreat.

20 Saladin learns of the situation and sends several detachments to support the false ambush but, because it is too late for a major battle, accepts that his plan has failed.

21 Seeing Saladin's reinforcements, the Franks recognize the danger of their position, kill their captives and retreat to Tyre.

22 The following day (25 July) Saladin learns that one of his elite mamluk soldiers, Aybak, is missing. The wounded man is found amongst the dead, and, as Baha al-Din recalls: 'They took him up and carried him to the camp in that state and God restored him to full health.'

On another occasion, 'During one of the fiercest engagements on the plain of Acre the Muslims were routed, even the centre and the sultan's guard. The drums and the banner fell, while he, God be pleased with him, stood firm in a small troop. He had them withdraw to the hill, to rally the men and to stop their flight, to shame them into resuming the battle. He persisted until the Muslim army was victorious over the enemy that day.' In the end Saladin could not save Acre from the massive forces of the Third Crusade, which was under the equally inspirational leadership of King Richard of England and King Philip Augustus of France. The exhausted garrison surrendered, without Saladin's authorization, on 12 July 1191.

For Saladin the rest of the campaign was a defensive holding operation. The only significant battle, occurring outside the coastal city of Arsuf on 7 September 1191, was a tactical defeat, though certainly not the catastrophe described by Crusader chroniclers and those historians who rely excessively upon them. In fact Saladin again attempted one of the classic moves advised in traditional medieval Islamic books on military

Right: One of the most remarkable objects uncovered by archaeologists in the ruins of the medieval city of Raqqa in north-eastern Syria was a large, late 12th- or early 13th-century ceramic statue of a horseman fighting a serpent. (Syrian National Museum, Damascus; author's photograph)

leadership. This was an attack on a marching army late in the day, at the moment when it was hopefully becoming disorganized as its vanguard approached a place where the army intended to make camp.

It was far from an uncoordinated assault. Seen from the Crusader side, Saladin's army was arrayed in a regular and clearly impressive manner, as described by the anonymous author of the *Chronicle of the Third Crusade*:

They were well drawn up with so many emblems fixed to their lances, so many standards, so many banners with a variety of details, so many lines appropriately divided into troops and troops arranged in companies that there seemed at a guess to be more than 20,000 armed Turks approaching in order... Certain people were assigned to go before the amirs sounding trumpets and clarions; others held horns, others flutes, tambourines, rattles or cymbals; others had other instruments for making a noise. They were assigned to the single task of raising shouts and horrible yells.[8]

The presence of a military figure in this Arabic translation of an ancient Greek work on the medicinal properties of plants, made in Iraq in 1224, might indicate that the properties in question helped heal wounds. (Freer Gallery, inv. no. 53.91r, Washington; author's photograph)

Opposite: Saladin's military architects designed a long wall that stretched from the Citadel of Cairo to the river Nile, driving right through the ruins of the earlier suburb of Fustat. (Author's photograph)

In reality the latter may have included those reciters of the Koran who had accompanied Muslim armies since the earliest days, whilst others shouted Islamic battle cries to fire the men with religious enthusiasm.

However, Saladin's attempt to halt the Crusaders outside Arsuf failed, and so he adopted a strictly defensive strategy. One of his most painful decisions was to render Ascalon indefensible and thus hinder the Crusaders' use of it as a base from which to invade northern Egypt. The city was therefore evacuated while sections of its fortifications were razed by specialist units of miners and masons. Saladin furthermore ordered his brother al-'Adil in Egypt to take personal authority over the fleet, strengthening the fortifications of Dumyat and evacuating all women and children from the town. The nearby island city of Tinnis was entirely emptied of its civilian population, marking the end of that once-flourishing commercial centre.

The defences of Ramla were similarly demolished, as was the massive church in Lydda, which could have been converted into a strongpoint. Meanwhile, Saladin established his own camp at al-Natrun on 29 September and started a prolonged, though intermittent, process of negotiations with the enemy. These did not stop the fighting and Muslim troops continued to harass the invaders, their communications and their supply lines wherever they could. Saladin was now painfully aware that his tired army was impatient to return to its homes.

---

8   Anon. (tr. Nicholson, H. J.), *Chronicle of the Third Crusade* (Aldershot, 2001) p. 248.

In fact the majority were demobilized on 12 December, after which the sultan and his own personal regiments pulled back to Jerusalem.

The massive Crusader invasion, initially led by the three strongest monarchs in Western Christendom, had been fought to a standstill. A huge Christian effort had regained only a small part of the old Kingdom of Jerusalem and had hardly even come in sight of the holy city of Jerusalem. On the other hand Saladin's realm was exhausted militarily, financially and perhaps even spiritually.

Having failed to get much support from his Muslim neighbours, Saladin decided to seek a peace that preserved his remaining gains. His most sympathetic biographers presented this strategic decision in a positive light, though some of Saladin's critics were less charitable. Baha al-Din was a great admirer of the sultan and according to him: 'He continued to resist them steadfastly, though they were in great numbers, until the weakness of the Muslims became evident to him. Then he made peace at their request, for their weakness and losses were greater, although they were expecting reinforcements and we expected none.'

An agreement was finally signed between 1 and 3 September 1192. On 9 October King Richard set sail homewards, and on 4 November Saladin returned to Damascus. The Third Crusade was over.

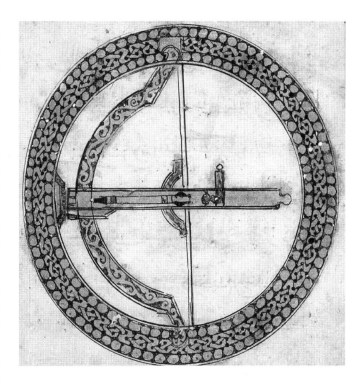

A crossbow attached to the interior of a shield was one of the bizarre weapons described and illustrated in a book about military equipment written for Saladin by al-Tarsusi. (Bodleian Library, Ms. Hunt 261, f.117, Oxford)

OPPOSING COMMANDERS

Shawar Ibn Mujir al-Sa'idi

'Iranians leaving the castle of Furud', an episode in the epic Persian *Shahnamah* poem on a late 12th-century Kashan-ware tile, probably from a palace. (Museum of Fine Arts, Boston; author's photograph)

History has not been kind to Shawar Ibn Mujir. He was one in the line of military *wazirs* who dominated the Fatimid army, state and to a great extent even the caliph himself from the 1130s onwards. They are usually regarded as symbols of the degeneracy of the Fatimid state. According to the Israeli historian Yaacov Lev, the weakening of the Isma'ili Shia imam or caliph in relation to these chief *wazirs* stemmed from changes in the structure of the Fatimid army. These were above all the introduction of an *'iqta* system of military fiefs – taken even further by Saladin – and alterations in the recruitment patterns of the *'abid*, which were largely Sudanese infantry regiments of the caliphal guard.

Shawar first came to prominence as an Arab governor of Sa'id, the part of Upper Egypt from which he got the name al-Sa'idi. His main support base was amongst the local people of this region and especially the Bedouin Arab tribes, who remained a powerful force in Egypt, especially in the south where they formed a local aristocracy. With this southern-Egyptian army at his back, Shawar rebelled against the existing *wazir*, Ruzzayk, whom he overthrew, and was then himself installed as *wazir* by the virtually powerless young Fatimid Caliph al-'Adid in December 1162. In the chaotic conditions of Egypt at the time, Shawar had to rely upon several other powerful men, including his ruthless sons Tayy and al-Kamil, his chief military commanders Yahya Ibn al-Khayyat and 'Abd al-Rahman al-Baysani from Palestine and also upon a powerful political figure in the Fatimid court, the Nubian eunuch al-Mu'tamin al-Khilafah.

Although he was only *wazir* of the Fatimid state for a few years, Shawar attempted to govern an almost impossible situation. Both the Crusader Kingdom of Jerusalem and Nur al-Din, the increasingly powerful ruler of Syria, wanted to dominate and perhaps even take over Egypt. Shawar's own preference seems to have been for an alliance with the Crusaders, though when this failed he is said to have considered a marriage alliance between Saladin, who was Nur al-Din's representative in Egypt, and his own daughter. This rumour was nevertheless strongly denied by all concerned.

At various times Shawar attempted to ally himself with, and to fight against, both Sunni Muslim Syrians and Catholic Christian Crusaders. Despite his best efforts, he failed, and as a result was almost inevitably overthrown in August 1163 by a new *wazir*, Dirgham. Shawar regained power not long after and remained *wazir* until his assassination in 1169. Unfortunately Shawar was remembered not only for his various military defeats, notably by Shirkuh and Saladin at the battle of al-Babayn, but also for destroying much of his own capital in 1168. In fact this destruction was almost certainly exaggerated by chroniclers eager to denigrate the unfortunate Shawar. Nevertheless it illustrated a degree of ruthlessness or perhaps desperation on his part.

The Crusaders had taken and sacked the fortified town of Bilbays on the eastern edge of the Nile Delta before pressing on to attack Cairo itself. Here the old capital of Fustat, on the southern edge of the Fatimid caliphal palace-city of al-Qahira (Cairo) is said to have been burned on Shawar's orders in order to stop its wealth falling into enemy hands. Historians have tended to see the destruction of Fustat in November 1168 as a seminal moment in the history of the Crusades. However, recent archaeological studies indicate that the devastation was by no means as extensive as once thought. There had been several fires over a number of years and the entire urban area had probably been in decline since the appalling Egyptian famines and plagues of 1066–72. An area along the east bank of the river Nile continued to flourish but it seems that any revival or expansion of the inhabited area was southward and westward, onto land left by a gradual shifting of the Nile itself. The fate of the eastern quarters remains unclear and the ruins through which Saladin later built his defensive wall had probably been abandoned by

The ruler on this minai-ware bowl from 12th- or early 13th-century Iran carries an animal-headed mace. Another man has a mail shirt beneath a lamellar cuirass while the man on the left probably wears a form of cloth-covered armour. (Museum of Fine Arts, Boston, author's photograph)

this time. Furthermore, the complete burning of 12th-century Fustat would have had a cataclysmic economic and social impact for which there is no real evidence.

Mas'ud Ibn Mawdud Izz al-Din

Because Saladin was such a dominant figure in the Islamic regions facing the Crusader states in the latter part of the 12th century, his contemporaries and rivals have tended to be overlooked. Many of them also became his allies, having failed to contain the expansion of Saladin's power. One such leader was Mas'ud Ibn Mawdud Izz al-Din, also known as Mas'ud I. He was one of the great 'Imad al-Din Zangi's grandsons, ruling a Zangid state centred upon the northern Iraqi city of Mosul from 1180 to 1193. The Syrian branch of the Zangid dynasty had been absorbed by the Mosul branch soon after the death of Nur al-Din, but this brought them up against the rising power of Saladin. Although the Egyptian sultan twice failed to conquer Mosul, once in 1182 and again in 1185, Mas'ud Ibn Mawdud did accept his nominal suzerainty in 1183.

Even before he became ruler of Mosul, Mas'ud Ibn Mawdud Izz al-Din had faced Saladin in battle. This was, in fact, a particularly interesting clash at the Horns of Hama, the name of which seemed to be a foretaste of Saladin's greater victory at the Horns of Hattin. It was fought on 13 April 1175 and pitted Saladin's largely Egyptian-based army, plus troops from recently conquered Damascus, against the Zangid army of Mosul from northern Iraq. Generally speaking it seems that troops from Syria, and perhaps also from Egypt, had greater military experience than those of the regions ruled by Mosul and its allies.

According to some sources the army of Mosul had been arrayed by 'Izz al-Din, the brother of Ghazi II Sayf al-Din who then ruled Mosul. The latter was also advised by a senior amir named Zulfandir. At first it looked as if both sides had deployed in a highly conventional manner, each with a centre and two wings. However, while Saladin commanded his own centre, he had also hidden reserves behind a nearby *tall*, or small conical hill, which marked the site of an ancient settlement. According to the contemporary chronicler Ibn al-Athir:

> They met on 19 Ramadan [13 April 1175] near the city of Hama at a place called the Horns of Hama. Zulfandir was ignorant of military matters and fighting, unacquainted with their practice, in addition to being a coward, although he had been granted good fortune and favour by Sayf al-Din [ruler of Mosul]. When the two sides met, Sayf al-Din's force did not hold firm but fled, every man looking out for himself. Sayf al-Din's brother, 'Izz al-Din, stood firm after the rout of his men. When Saladin saw his steadfastness, he said, 'Either this is the bravest of men or he has no knowledge of warfare'. He ordered his men [probably the hidden reserves] to charge him, which they did and drove him from his position. Their rout then became complete.[9]

---

9   Ibn al-Athir, op. cit., p. 236.

Other descriptions of this one-sided battle state that Saladin's troops forced the enemy away from 'their baggage, their beasts and their infantry', which seems to be another reference to the sudden flanking attack by hidden reserves. Large numbers of prisoners were taken, and Saladin followed the advice of generations of Muslim military theoreticians by not allowing them to be harmed. He was fully aware that these men might well be future allies, or even members of his own army. Such large numbers of horses were also captured at the Horns of Hama that Saladin's foot soldiers reportedly became mounted infantry.

Reynald of Châtillon

Sometimes known as 'The Elephant of Christ', Reynald of Châtillon tends to be seen either as a romantic hero who showed astonishing strategic vision, or as a bloodthirsty bandit warped by years as a prisoner-of-war in a Turkish dungeon. He was undoubtedly brave and good looking. Having arrived in the Crusader states from France without wealth or many followers in 1153, Reynald of Châtillon won the hand of Princess Constance of Antioch. However, he was captured by the Muslims and spent the years 1161–75 as a prisoner in Aleppo. This left him with a burning hatred for Islam, but also a deep knowledge of the culture of the Islamic Middle East. In subsequent years the Muslims were correct in viewing Arnat, as they knew Reynald, as their most dedicated foe.

By the time of Reynald of Châtillon's release, his wife Constance was dead, so he promtly married the heiress to the Crusader lordship of Oultrejordain. There he established a powerful state-within-a-state, perhaps hoping to one day be as independent as the County of Tripoli or even the Principality of Antioch.

Of all his astonishing military campaigns, none was more remarkable than the one he launched, but did not personally lead, during the winter of 1182–83. According to the Crusader chronicler Ernoul, Reynald had five galleys whereas other sources seem to indicate a small squadron of between five and ten ships, probably of varied types taken as prefabricated parts to the Red Sea.

The choice of the port of 'Aydhab, close to what is now the border between Egypt and Sudan, as the primary target for Reynald's fleet showed a detailed knowledge of the trade and pilgrim routes. It is also one of many factors that prove the raiders had local support from sailors or merchants with detailed local knowledge. If Reynald's raids had succeeded they might effectively have split the Islamic world in two. They would certainly have had a huge impact upon Muslim trade with

One of two medieval helmets made from crocodile skin, found in Nubia near the frontier between Egypt and Sudan. These were probably typical of the sort of protection worn by the Nubian raiding forces that menaced southern Egypt during the early years of Saladin's reign. (Staatliche Museen Berlin; J. Laurentias photograph)

India and might even have opened up direct links between Mediterranean Europe and the Indian Ocean three centuries before the great Age of Discovery. Saladin probably had more immediate concerns, such as the possibility of Reynald linking up with lingering pro-Fatimid elements in Upper Egypt, Nubia and Yemen, not to mention the threat of a real (rather than imaginary) alliance between the Christian Crusader states and the Christian African kingdoms of Nubia and Ethiopia. In reality Reynald of Châtillon's astonishing strategic vision went beyond his military capabilities. The raids failed, and only served to reinforce Saladin's determination to crush the Crusaders once and for all. They also contributed to the sultan's personal anger with the Lord of Oultrejordain, whom he is credited with killing – or at least striking the first blow – after the battle of Hattin.

King Amalric of Jerusalem

Amalric was the son of Fulk of Anjou and Queen Melisende of Jerusalem, and the younger brother of King Baldwin III. His first significant position of authority was as Count of Jaffa, which he held for only one year because he quarrelled with his brother, the king. Baldwin restored the lands of Jaffa and added those of Ascalon around 1154. Amalric himself came to the throne nine years later and spent the greater part of his reign attempting with some success to strengthen the Crown of Jerusalem financially, legally, politically and militarily. In fact he is widely seen as one of the Crusader Kingdom's more successful rulers.

Much of his attention was focused upon Egypt, where the declining Fatimid Caliphate held out the possibilty of huge wealth and territorial expansion. However, Nur al-Din of Syria was similarly aware of Egypt's potential and this resulted in a remarkable series of campaigns for control of Egypt by these competing rulers. For King Amalric they were often undertaken

Amongst the most important recent discoveries to shed light on Middle Eastern Islamic military equipment from the time of the Crusades is a hoard of material from a forgotten stairwell in the Citadel of Damascus. (Syrian National Museum Conservation Department, Damascus; author's photograph)

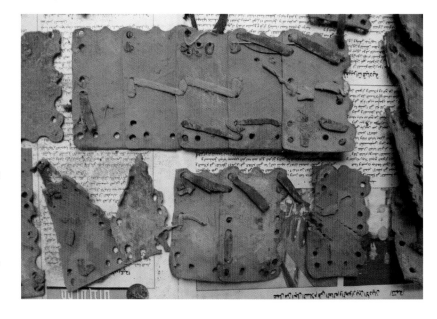

in alliance with the Byzantine Empire and included a number of bitter sieges. For example, after Shirkuh and Saladin's victory over the army of the Fatimid and Kingdom of Jerusalem alliance at the battle of al-Babayn, Shirkuh withdrew to Alexandria, which was his main base in Egypt.

Fearing that food supplies might still reach Shirkuh's army from southern Egypt, King Amalric left some ships in Cairo before heading for Alexandria. He then made camp between Kum Trugah and Damanhur, some 60km from the great Egyptian seaport. Perhaps he was waiting for scouts to report on the situation at Alexandria or perhaps he feared that the water level in the Alexandria Canal was too low for his ships. Certainly the level of the Nile continued to drop until the annual Nile flood. Meanwhile Shirkuh decided to split his forces and left Saladin to defend Alexandria while he himself returned south with the bulk of the army.

Once King Amalric knew that Shirkuh had slipped past him, he set off in pursuit, joining his ally the Fatimid *wazir* Shawar in Cairo. The King of Jerusalem then had second thoughts when he learned that there was fear of famine in Alexandria and so returned to press the siege. It lasted from early May to 4 August and involved a close bombardment by mangonels as well as a tight blockade. Nevertheless the local inhabitants continued to support Saladin and his troops. Many foreign merchants also helped in the defence of Alexandria while Nur al-Din launched diversionary raids against the Crusader states in Syria. Far to Amalric's rear, Shirkuh continued to campaign in Upper Egypt but eventually had to return north and start negotiations for a truce. The situation in Alexandria was now serious and consequently Shirkuh and the Syrians made the most concessions.

Saladin's immediate concern was to get his sick and injured safely back to Syria, and according to a study by the Egyptian historian Professor Omran: 'He asked Amalric to let him have them taken off by ship, but when they reached Acre those who had recovered were made to work in the sugar-plantations and it was only after Amalric had intervened in person that they were allowed to depart for Damascus.'[10]

In fact the failure of Amalric's Egyptian plans resulted in it becoming the base for a new and even more threatening power, namely that of Saladin. Amalric died in July 1174, only a few weeks after Nur al-Din, and his heir was a child who already suffered from leprosy, the tragic King Baldwin IV.

King Richard of England

King Richard I of England, known as Coeur de Lion or the 'Lion Hearted', was actually French. Born in 1157, he learned the skills of administration and of war as governor of the vast fiefdom of Aquitaine on behalf of his father King Henry II. However, Richard of Poitou as he was then widely known, was not a dutiful son. He rebelled against his father in 1173–74 and again in 1189, but that same year King Henry II died and Richard became ruler of England and a great part of south-western France.

---

10 Omran, M. S., 'King Almaric and the Siege of Alexandria, 1167', in Edbury, P. W. (ed.), *Crusade and Settlement* (Cardiff, 1985) p. 195.

Medieval Islamic art often shows military figures on foot, but they were usually dismounted cavalrymen. (Keir Collection, London)

Richard's motivation, like his sexuality, has been the subject of heated academic debate. Like his great rival, King Philip Augustus of France, King Richard used crusading as a means of enhancing his own reputation. In fact he 'took the cross' by declaring in public his intention of going on crusade to regain the Holy Land from Saladin before his father Henry died. Although this proclamation earned King Richard respect within his own realm, it would be probably be wrong to see it merely as a political ploy or a warlike adventure. As the historian D. Carpenter wrote: 'For someone often prey to a morbid sense of his own sinfulness, the spiritual benefits of the crusade, with the promise of remission of all sins, were compelling. So was the chance to exercise martial talents ... not against fellow Christians but against the infidels.'[11] Without doubt it was King Richard of England rather than King Philip of France who welded the disparate forces of the Third Crusade into a potent fighting force under his leadership, largely through his obvious charisma and considerable knowledge of warfare.

On the other hand, Richard took the ruthlessness that he had learned in Europe with him on his crusade. When the exhausted garrison of Acre surrendered in July 1191, ransom arrangements for the captured men were agreed. However, there were delays in payment so King Richard had the great majority of prisoners and their families slaughtered in full view of Saladin's scouts. The latter tried to intervene but were too few to save their comrades, while the bulk of Saladin's army was too far away to help.

After his victory outside Arsuf, Richard clearly hoped to advance against Jerusalem. Here, however, Saladin had the fortifications repaired, fully manned and put into a state of defence. Both leaders sought to inspire their men by setting a personal example. Whereas Richard was frequently in the front line of battle, Saladin carried masonry for the defences of Jerusalem on the saddle of his horse. Clearly both sides suffered badly from the winter, but things seem to have been worse for the Crusaders, especially when Richard attempted to advance towards Jerusalem through rain and mud. Harassed by the Muslims and unable to go farther, Richard eventually ordered a withdrawal on 8 January 1192.

The final months of the Third Crusade witnessed some tactically interesting skirmishing and ambushes, but military operations were now on a small scale. Diplomacy and negotiation became more important, and these were fields in which Saladin held mastery over Richard.

11 D. Carpenter, *The Struggle for Mastery, Britain 1066–1284* (London, 2003) p. 246.

INSIDE THE MIND

Saladin clearly used religion to strengthen his political, military and diplomatic position, but there is no reason to suppose that his personal piety was anything other than genuine. Nor was there a reason for his faith and his ambitions to clash. Indeed they generally went hand in hand, as when, in 1189, Saladin travelled to Jerusalem to celebrate the Islamic 'Feast of Sacrifice' while at the same time emphasizing the religious significance of a city he had regained for Islam. On the other hand Saladin's awareness that Jerusalem was similarly important to his Crusader opponents probably made peace negotiations more complicated. Nor was Saladin superstitious, unlike so many Muslim and Christian rulers of his day. In September 1186, for example, he refused to believe a popular astrological prediction that the world would end in a universal flood and whirlwind caused by a conjunction of six planets in the zodiacal sign of Libra.

Jihad was central to Saladin's propaganda war against rival Muslim rulers, but he went beyond mere words and shed a great deal of Muslim blood in his campaigns to unite the Islamic Middle East against the Crusader menace. Saladin also struggled to unite the Muslims of the region in religious loyalty to the Sunni caliph in Baghdad. Despite these efforts Saladin often found the 'Abbasid caliphs unhelpful, largely because the caliphs themselves wanted to lead the jihad politically as well as spiritually. Whereas Caliph al-Mustadi (1170–80) had generally been neutral, his successor al-Nasir (1180–1225) was much more suspicious. To make matters worse, al-Nasir was in direct competition with Saladin to take control of Zangid Mosul in northern Iraq, and during this period the 'Abbasid Caliphate re-emerged as a significant regional power with a large territory.

Like Nur al-Din, his predecessor in Syria, Saladin extended the struggle between Sunni and Shia Islam into the fields of art and architecture, although most such cultural patronage came from leading members of his army, administration and family rather than Saladin himself. As a result there was a great increase in the number of mosques and *madrasah* schools, particularly in the cities, under Saladin and his Ayyubid successors. Syrian *madrasahs* of this

Part of a broken late 12th- or early 13th-century Egyptian ceramic bowl showing men in a galley. Though very stylized, this little picture nevertheless illustrates a form of oared ship that was essentially the same as those used by the Byzantine Empire and by the Mediterranean states of Western Europe. (Museum of Islamic Art, inv. no. 5335.65, Cairo; author's photograph)

One of the rarest but also most damaged items to be found in the hoard of military material from a forgotten stairwell in the Citadel of Damascus are parts of a shield made of a spiral of cane bound with cotton. (Syrian National Museum Conservation Department, Damascus; author's photograph)

period often contained the tombs of their founders and Saladin's Ayyubid successors would, for example, use the *madrasah*-tomb of Saladin for their own Friday prayers.

Family solidarity was a central feature of Saladin's political and military system. For example, the chronicler Ibn al-Azraq of Mayyafariqin was in Damascus during the winter of 1170–71 where he saw a huge caravan set out, taking Saladin's brother Shams al-Dawla Turan Shah, his family and dependants to Egypt where Saladin was starting the process of building a family power base. It was said to consist of over 70,000 camels with up to three women and five small children riding each animal. However, the solidarity of Saladin's extensive family was sometimes more theoretical than real, the sultan having particular problems with his brave and efficient but independent-minded nephew Taqi al-Din. According to Ibn al-'Athir the younger man was noted for his skill in the art of fortifications and he was clearly admired by his uncle Saladin. Nevertheless Taqi al-Din virtually deserted the struggle against the Third Crusade to pursue his own ambitions in eastern Turkey and northern Syria.

Marriage alliances between elite families were as important in the medieval Islamic world as they were in medieval Europe, and Saladin certainly made use of them. In 1176 his marriage to 'Ismat al-Din Khatun, the daughter of Mu'in al-Din Ünür of Damascus and widow of Nur al-Din, provided Saladin with a personal link with two rulers who had preceded him. Similarly, Saladin sought to cement the loyalty of important military leaders such as the Turk Muzaffar al-Din Gökböri, who had governed Irbil in northern Iraq since the age of 14. In 1186 Saladin arranged the marriage between his younger sister al-Sitt Rabi'a Khatun and Gökböri. Within months that Turkish warrior repaid Saladin handsomely at the battle of Hattin. It is also worth noting that the women in Saladin's family played a role in the cultural struggles of the time. For example, shortly after Saladin retook Jerusalem from the Crusader Kingdom, Rabi'a Khatun established a *madrasah* there, which was intended for Nasih al-Din ibn al-Hanbali, a teacher and leading member of Saladin's entourage. Rabi'a Khatun then attended his inaugural lecture, seated behind a curtain.

WHEN WAR IS DONE

'The men of war were occupied with their war, the people lived for peace. The war did not involve the people or the merchants.' With these words Ibn Jubayr summed up his view of the situation in Syria around the time of the Third Crusade. That epic but inconclusive campaign was followed by half a century of relative peace. Western European Christendom would launch further Crusades, usually directed against Egypt, but apart from successfully defeating these assaults most Ayyubid military energies were absorbed in petty squabbles between competing members of the ruling dynasty. The Third Crusade had taught Saladin, his successors and the rulers of the Crusader states that prolonged conflict damaged both sides. Nevertheless all recognized the need for military preparedness during a period of 'medieval cold war'.

The prolonged struggle against the Crusaders had put huge strains upon Saladin's realm, especially in Egypt where a lack of gold undermined the currency. The Nubian gold mines upon which ancient Egypt had relied were virtually exhausted. Western Sudan was the main source of gold for North Africa and much of Europe, but this was largely denied to Saladin by his North African rivals, the Muwahhidun. Furthermore, the Crusaders attempted to undermine Egyptian currency by minting imitation dinar gold coins with a debased value. For a while tokens made of glass paste were even issued by Saladin's government as a form of temporary currency.

Surprisingly, perhaps, the Egyptian economy was not particularly affected by Saladin's decision to replace the old Fatimid aristocracy of large landowners and administrators by a new and more direct system of 'iqta fiefs. It also says a great deal for the smoothness of Saladin's reforms that the new regime was able to crush occasional Fatimid resistance without seriously damaging agricultural production. There was a massive new emphasis on fortification, but the building boom that characterized Saladin's reign went well beyond repairing towns and suburbs devastated by decades of war. Saladin's campaigns

Saladin had small fortified khans built along some vital or exposed trade routes, this being the Khan al-'Arus just north of Damascus. (Author's photograph)

Islamic art of this period tended to illustrate peaceful rather than military scenes. One of the most popular was a man and woman in conversation, often sharing a drink of wine despite the Islamic prohibition on alcohol. This 12th- or early 13th-century minai-ware bowl was made in western Iran. (Reza Abbasi Museum, Tehran; author's photograph)

also created a massive demand for arms, armour, harnesses, clothing and ships. For example the Egyptian fleet, which almost disappeared in the final years of the Fatimid Caliphate, increased in strength to about 60 fighting galleys and around 20 transport vessels by 1179.

Prolonged warfare hardly interrupted trade and Saladin put a great deal of investment into roads, bridges and fortified khans. Once again the observant Ibn Jubayr sheds light on this process, describing a khan built by Saladin between Damascus and Nabk – probably Khan al-'Arus: 'It is the zenith of strength and handsomeness, with iron doors after the fashion of the builders of the khans on this road and in accordance with the attention with which they fortify them. Inside the khan is running water which flows through underground conduits to a fountain in the middle.'

While European historians tend to focus on trade in the Mediterranean, the maritime trade of the Red Sea and Indian Ocean were equally important for Saladin. Following Reynald of Châtillon's devastating raids, Saladin closed the Red Sea to non-Muslim merchants and shipping. As a result Muslim merchants known as the Karimis came to dominate the trade routes to India, excluding the Jewish and Christian merchants of Egypt, Palestine and Yemen who had previously played an important role.

Much has been made of Saladin's reforms to the systems of government in Egypt and Syria but this should not be overstated. The question of whether Saladin is best described as the leader of a war-band or as a true territorial ruler also remains a matter of debate. As the historian P. M. Holt has pointed out, he was in many respects very similar to contemporary rulers like the Normans of southern Italy and Sicily, or the Angevins of England and much of France. Like them, he ruled two distinct and very different territories and did so by using a 'peripatetic administrative nucleus'. Saladin also inherited a bureaucracy and relied upon a system of patronage to maintain the loyalty of those men, largely military, upon whom he relied. Furthermore, it is easy to exaggerate the effectiveness and efficiency of the diwan government departments of Saladin's administration, and indeed those of his Muslim rivals. Such governments tended to rely upon personal allegiance and loyal companionship rather than professional bureaucracies.

Two *qubbat* domed tomb chambers at Sinjar in northern Iraq. The one on the right is that of Zainab, and partially dates from the early 13th century. The Sinjar area was prosperous and militarily important in Saladin's day, but never recovered from the Mongol devastation of the mid-13th century. (Yusuf al-Kurdi photograph)

This is not, of course, to say that a professional bureaucracy did not exist in Saladin's realm. He inherited one from the Fatimid Caliphate, though it was not as efficient as sometimes claimed. Amongst those who served the Fatimids and then Saladin was the chronicler al-Qadi al-Fadil who had once supervised the Fatimid diwan al-Jaysh, or 'army ministry'. 'Imad al-Din al-Isfahani had a different background and his career showed how an elite with administrative skills moved around the Middle East. It also highlighted how rulers befriended such vital bureaucrats. 'Imad al-Din actually described his own working relationship with Saladin: 'If he needed to draw up an official letter or divulge some confidential plan, he would sit me down and dictate the main outlines. Then I would leave and spend the night composing the letters. Early next day I would go and present them to him. If he decided to add or change something in the content he would bring my attention to the paragraph and tell me which passages. I would stay until I had put it all in order. When he had approved them in their final form, he would sign them and say "Let us send them off without delay".'[12] Indeed, 'Imad al-Din's view of his own role indicates that he saw his pen and Saladin's sword as almost equal partners in the struggle against the Crusaders.

Saladin did not live long after his peace agreement with King Richard of England. He seems to have been exhausted from years of hard campaigning. Nevertheless the death of Saladin came as a shock and was widely lamented. An anonymous poet quoted by Abu Shama wrote: 'The sword of God, always hanging above His enemies, has returned to its sheath... In losing its defender, Islam remains like a mother who weeps for her only son.' The contemporary traveller and chronicler 'Abd al-Latif al-Baghdadi was more prosaic: 'This was the only instance of a king's death that was truly mourned by the people.'

The 'Sword of Saladin' was found in his tomb in Damascus. An inscription on its blade states that it was made for his father Najm al-Din Ayyub. (Askeri Muse, inv. no. 2355, Istanbul, author's photograph)

12 Richards, D. S., "Imad al-Din al-Isfahani; Administrator, Litterateur and Historian', in Shatzmiller, M. (ed.), *Crusaders and Muslims in Twelfth Century Syria* (Leiden, 1993) p. 139.

A LIFE IN WORDS

Saladin's life and achievements were viewed very differently in the Islamic and Christian worlds. Even so, Western European Latin Catholic opinions of the great Islamic hero changed quite quickly. The anonymous *Chronicle of the Third Crusade* was written immediately after the event, by a participant who reflected on the widespread horror at the fall of Jerusalem to Muslim 'infidels'. It blamed Saladin's success on the failings of the Crusader states: 'The Lord saw that the land of His Nativity, the place of His Passion, had fallen into the filthy abyss. Therefore He spurned His Inheritance, permitting the rod of His Fury, Saladin, to rage and exterminate the obstinate people.'

The epic quality of the struggle that followed was recognized on all sides and although the sources are not as apocalyptic as those dealing with the First Crusade, they were more emotionally charged than most that recounted later Crusades. In this sense the Arabic texts are particularly interesting as they reflected a change from near euphoria after the battle of Hattin to growing despair as Muslim forces fell back before the Third Crusade. Eventually Saladin fought King Richard to a standstill, but this could not disguise the fact that he was now on the defensive. During the prolonged siege of Acre Saladin almost used up his military, naval and economic resources – perhaps also exhausting himself.

By the start of the 20th century the *madrasah* or college containing Saladin's tomb in Damascus had fallen into decay. When Kaiser Wilhelm II visited the city in 1908 he had the tomb restored at German expense. (Author's photograph)

Not surprisingly, Western accounts highlighted any evidence that Saladin admired the leaders of the Third Crusade. When Bishop Hubert of Salisbury made his pilgrimage to Jerusalem, the Muslim ruler told him: 'It is well known to us that the king [Richard I of England] has the greatest prowess and boldness, but he frequently hurls himself into danger imprudently, I do not say foolishly... Wherever and in whatever kinds of countries I may be the distinguished prince, I would much prefer to be enriched with an abundance of wisdom and moderation, rather than with boldness and lack of self control.'[13] In the eyes of westerners Saladin was, in fact, already seen as a wise, but crafty and not particularly brave, leader.

13 Anon. (tr. Nicholson, H. J.), *Chronicle of the Third Crusade* (Aldershot, 2001) p. 378.

Saladin's tomb lies beneath the small, fluted and red-painted dome immediately in front of the northern minaret of the Umayyad Great Mosque in this photograph. (Author's photograph)

Muslim opinions of Saladin were also varied, with chroniclers being divided into pro-Ayyubid and pro-Zangid camps. Most tried to hide their political loyalties but these occasionally burst through, as when 'Imad al-Din al-Isfahani said of the Islamic year 583 AH (12 March 1187 to 2 March 1188): 'It is the second Hijra of Islam, but this time to Jerusalem [the first having been the Prophet Muhammad's move from Mecca to Madina]… It can justly be regarded as the beginning of a new era, since it marks a turning point in the course of Islam.'

The chronicler Ibn al-'Athir actually fought for Saladin against the Crusaders and was quite open about Muslim mistakes. These included Saladin's failure to attack Guy de Lusignan's force before it reached Acre in August 1189: 'Were it not for the fact that the army followed the opinion of Salah al-Din in their manner of arrangement and fighting before they reached Acre, they would have achieved their aim and blocked [the enemy] from it.'

Writing about Saladin's enthusiasm for war against the Crusaders, Baha al-Din was more supportive: 'In his love for the Jihad on the path of God he shunned his womenfolk, his children, his homeland, his home and all his pleasures, and for this world he was content to dwell in the shade of his tent with the winds blowing through it left and right.' Baha al-Din was equally impressed by Saladin as a commander: 'I have never at all seen him consider the enemy too numerous nor exaggerate their strength. However, he

The faces in this early 13th-century Iraqi or Syrian copy of the *maqamat* by al-Hariri have been smudged out. Both the men and the horse have also been decapitated by black lines drawn long after the manuscript was made. Nevertheless the costumes and the horse's saddle are shown in interesting detail. (Institute of Oriental Studies, C-23, f.174, St Petersburg, via V. A. Livskity)

was sometimes deep in thought and forward planning, dealing with all departments and arranging what was required for each without any onset of bad temper or anger.'

Nevertheless, resentment occasionally surfaced in later chronicles and is seen in the words of the leader of an Arab revolt against the Mamluk takeover of Egypt in 1250: 'We are the lords of the land. We are more worthy to rule than the Mamluks. It was enough to serve the Ayyubids [the dynasty established by Saladin], who were rebels and took the land by force, and they [the Mamluks] are only the slaves of the rebels.'[14]

The depth of Western European ignorance and misunderstanding of the Islamic world at the time of the Third Crusade is apparent in the anonymous *Chronicle of the Third Crusade*, which claimed that Saladin

> was from the nation of Mirmunaenus [a corruption of Amir al-Mu'minin or 'Leader of the Believers']. His parents were not descended from the nobility, but neither were they common people of obscure birth… Saladin collected illgotten gains for himself from a levy on the girls of Damascus. They were not allowed to practice as prostitutes unless they had obtained, at a price, a licence from him for carrying on the profession of lust. However, whatever he gained by pimping like this he paid back generously by funding plays. So through lavish giving to all their desires he won the mercenary favour of the common people.

Saladin's caution was similarly portrayed by Ambroise as cunning or treacherous. Admiration for the virtues of a few Saracen heroes only came to the fore in late 12th- and 13th-century texts, with Saladin being central to this altered image. Saladin was also given an unexpected position in the medieval Italian poet Dante's *Divine Comedy*. Not being a baptized Christian, he could not be placed in Paradise, but by 1300 Saladin's reputation was high enough for him to reside in Limbo rather than Hell: 'And there across that bright enamelled green, these ancient heroes were displayed to me… All these I saw, and there alone, apart, the sultan Saladin.'[15]

During the 19th century Saladin came to be seen by many in Europe as a heroic figure – the archetypal noble Saracen foe. As a result biographies such as that by Stanley Lane-Poole tended to be uncritical. Saladin's position in the pantheon of Muslim heroes has also inhibited critical scholarship in the modern Arab world, although several recent Arab historians have focused more upon Saladin's predecessors and have thus downgraded Saladin's own achievements. Similarly, the Arab world's adoption of Saladin as a role model in the struggle against Israel has encouraged several pro-Zionist historians to seek, consciously or otherwise, to debunk him.

In contrast, it is interesting to find that Western rather than Muslim historians have emphasized the legitimacy of Ayyubid rule compared to that of their supposedly 'slave' Mamluk successors. In most of the medieval Islamic

---

14 Holt, P. M., 'Saladin and his admirers: A biographical reassessment' in *Bulletin of the School of Oriental and African Studies*, 46 (1983) p. 130.

15 Dante (tr. Griffiths, E. & Reynolds, M.), *Dante in English* (London, 2005) Canto 4, Limbo, ll. pp. 118–29.

world, with the notable exception of the caliphate itself, legitimacy was a prize to be won like any other within the Islamic political system. Westerners, both medieval and modern, have also tended to see the fast-changing and complex political circumstances of the medieval Middle East as evidence of disorder, corruption and intrigue. The truth is that this part of the medieval world was politically more fluid, more meritocratic and to some extent more democratic than medieval Western Europe.

One disadvantage of this fluidity was that, despite his remarkable leadership and political skills, Saladin never succeeded in shaping Egypt and Syria into a single ideological, military or economic unit. This weakness became all too apparent after his death, when the Ayyubid realm or realms were little more than a collection of competing family fiefdoms.

It took an essentially unsympathetic, though hugely knowledgeable, modern biographer like Andrew Ehrenkreutz to highlight the shortcomings of Saladin's leadership:

> Despite his popular image following the great victory of Hattin and the glorious recovery of Jerusalem, Saladin's position as leader of the Muslim forces fighting the Crusaders was not too comfortable. As early as 1186, incidents with Nasir al-Din ibn Shirkuh and Taqi al-Din Umar had indicated that Saladin could not even trust his own relatives. Events at Tyre in 1187 had revealed that the rank and file was not overwhelmingly inspired by the jihad ideal which Saladin publicly embraced, and this self-asserted mandate itself had been repudiated in no uncertain terms by the caliph of Baghdad.[16]

A more sympathetic historian like P. M. Holt could still study the numerous recorded letters from Saladin's court and conclude that: 'The Saladin who emerges from these pages is no longer the confident and dedicated champion of Islam, even if he is not the anti-hero, disastrous to Egypt, depicted by Ehrenkreutz. The precarious nature of his position appears constantly. The jihad was a means of legitimising his authority.'

Lyons and Jackson similarly noted Saladin's precarious military position:

> A factor which has to be taken into account was the loose structure of his army. His allies had no reason to give him whole-hearted support. For his own emirs and professional soldiers he and his family were merely successful members of their own class; his dynasty was bolstered by no divine right of kings and the religious sanction it had claimed had been denied it by Baghdad. During the period of its expansion it had been profitable to join his side, but profit

When Saladin retook Jerusalem in 1187, he had a new pulpit of wood and ivory, which Nur al-Din had prepared for this day, placed in the al-Aqsa Mosque. Sadly, the passions that can still be aroused by the Crusades resulted in an Australian fanatic setting fire to the mosque in 1960 in the belief that this would hasten the Second Coming of Jesus, and destroying Nur al-Din's pulpit in the process. (Author's photograph)

16 Ehrenkreutz, A. S., *Saladin* (Albany, 1972) pp. 210–11

The Western European knightly class soon came to see Saladin as a worthy, though doomed, opponent of the Crusaders and a mythical combat between the Muslim hero and the English King Richard the Lionheart became a favourite theme in both literature and art.

and numbers were inextricably linked. If his military accounts began to show a loss, his numbers could be expected to diminish and his dynasty in its turn could be theatened by other muslim expansionists.[17]

Viewed dispassionately as the ruler of a frontier region facing powerful Crusader states, Saladin emerges as one in a series of leaders who used this situation to build a state through winning support as a defender of the region against its enemies. It was a process seen throughout history in many parts of the world. Nevertheless there is no denying that Saladin was more successful than most of his contemporaries in overcoming the factionalism that had for centuries undermined traditional Middle Eastern Muslim military systems, most obviously that of his Fatimid predecessors in Egypt. Therein, perhaps, lay the real secret of his success.

FURTHER READING

Ailes, M. J., 'The Admirable Enemy? Saladin and Saphadin in Ambroise's Estoire de la guerre sainte' in Housley, N. (ed.), *Knighthoods of Christ* (Aldershot, 2007) pp. 51–64

Aubé, P., *Un croisé contre Saladin: Renaud de Châtillon* (Paris, 2007)

Baldwin, M. W., *Raymond III of Tripolis and the Fall of Jerusalem (1140–1187)* (Princeton, 1936)

Barber, M., 'Frontier Warfare in the Latin Kingdom of Jerusalem: The Campaign at Jacob's Ford, 1178–9' in France, J. & Zajac, W. G. (eds.), *The Crusades and their sources: Essays Presented to Bernard Hamilton* (Aldershot, 1998) pp. 9–22

Brand, C. M., 'The Byzantines and Saladin, 1185–1192: Opponents of the Third Crusade', *Speculum*, 37 (1962) pp. 167–81

---

17 Lyons, M. C., & Jackson, D. E. P., *Saladin: The Politics of the Holy War* (Cambridge, 1982) p. 286.

A dramatic sculpture showing Saladin's victory at Hattin, now outside the Citadel of Damascus, also appears on the Syrian £200 bank note. (Author's collection)

DeVries, K., 'Disaster at Hattin, 1187: beginning of the end' in *Medieval History*, 5 (Jan. 2004) pp. 24–31

Edbury, P. W., 'The Battle of Hattin (4 July 1187) and its aftermath' in *The Conquest of Jerusalem and the Third Crusade: Sources in Translation* (Aldershot, 1998) pp. 158–163

Eddé, A-M., 'Quelques institutions militaires ayyoubides' in Vermeulen, U. & De Smet, D. (eds.), *Egypt and Syria in the Fatimid, Ayyubid and Mamluks Eras* (Leuven, 1995) pp. 163–74

Ehrenkreutz, A. S., 'The Place of Saladin in the Naval History of the Mediterranean Sea in the Middle Ages' in *Journal of the American Oriental Society,* 75 (1955) pp. 100–16

——, *Saladin* (New York, 1972)

Ehrlich, M., 'The Battle of Hattin: A Chronicle of a Defeat Foretold?' in *The Journal of Medieval Military History*, 5 (2007) pp. 16–32

Ellenblum, R., 'Frontier Activities: the Transformation of a Muslim Sacred Site into the Frankish Castle of Vadum Iacob' in *Crusades*, 2 (2003) pp. 83–97

Facey, W., 'Crusaders in the Red Sea: Reinaud de Chatillon's Raids of AD 1182–1183', in Starkey, J. C. M. (ed.), *People of the Red Sea: Proceedings of the Red Sea Project II, BAR International Series 1395* (Oxford, 2005) pp. 87–98

Gibb, H. A. R., 'The Armies of Saladin', *Cahiers d'Histoire Egyptienne*, 3 (1951) pp. 304–20

——, *The Life of Saladin, from the works of 'Imad ad-Din and Baha ad-Din* (Oxford, 1973)

Grillo, P. R., 'The Saladin material in the continuations of the First Crusade Cycle', in Dijk, H. van (ed.), *Aspects de l'epopee romane (Acts of the 13th International Congress of the Societe Rencesvals, Groningen, NL, Aug. 1994)* (Groningen, 1995) pp. 159–66

Hamblin, W. J., 'Saladin and Muslim Military Theory', in Kedar, B. Z. (ed.), *The Horns of Hattin* (Jerusalem, 1992) pp. 228–38

Herde, P., 'Historische Wendepunkte: die Schlachten von Hattin (3./4. Juli 1187) und 'Ain Galut (3. September 1260)', in Piana, M. (ed.), *Burgen und Städte der Kreuzzugzeit* (Petersberg, 2008) pp. 43–46

Holt, P. M., 'Saladin and his admirers: a biographical reassessment', *Bulletin of the School of Oriental and African Studies*, 46 (1983) pp. 235–39

Jackson, D. E. P., '1193–1993, an appreciation of the career of Saladin' in Vermeulen, U. & De Smet, D. (eds.), *Egypt and Syria in the Fatimid, Ayyubid and Mamluks Eras* (Leuven, 1995) pp. 219–28

Jubb, M., *The Legend of Saladin in Western Literature and Historiography* (Lewiston, 2000)

Katzir, Y., 'The Conquest of Jerusalem, 1099 and 1187: Historical Memory and Religious Typology', in Goss, V. P. (et al. eds.), *The Meeting of Two Worlds: Cultural Exchange between East and West during the Period of the Crusades* (Kalamazoo, 1986) pp. 103–13

Kedar, B. Z., 'A Western Survey of Saladin's Forces at the Siege of Acre', in Kedar, B. Z. (et al. eds.), *Montjoie: Studies in Crusade History in Honour of Hans Eberhard Mayer* (Aldershot, 1997) pp. 113–22

——, 'The Battle of Hattin Revisited' in Kedar, B. Z. (ed.), *The Horns of Hattin* (Jerusalem, 1992) pp. 190–207

Leiser, G. La V., 'The Crusader Raid in the Red Sea in 578/1182–83' in *Journal of the American Research Center in Egypt*, 14 (1977) pp. 87–100

Lev, Y., *Saladin in Egypt* (Leiden, 1988)

Lewis, B., 'Saladin and the Assassins,' in *Bulletin of the School of Oriental and African Studies*, 15 (1952) pp. 239–245

Ligato, G., 'Saladino e i prigonieri di guerra' in Cipollone, G. (ed.), *La Liberazione dei 'Captivi' tra Cristianità e Islam* (Vatican, 2000) pp. 649–654

Lilie, R-J., (tr. Morris, J. C. & Ridings, J. E.), *Byzantium and the Crusader states 1096–1204* (Oxford, 1993)

Lyons, M. C., & Jackson, *Saladin: The Politics of the Holy War* (Cambridge, 1982)

Magdalino, P., 'Isaac II, Saladin and Venice', in Shepard, J. (ed.), *The Expansion of Orthodox Europe: Byzantium, the Balkans and Russia* (Aldershot, 2007) pp. 93–106

Melville, C. P., & Lyons, M. C., 'Saladin's Hattin Letter' in Kedar, B. Z. (ed.), *The Horns of Hattin* (Jerusalem, 1992) pp. 208–12

Ménard, P., 'Les combattants en Terre sainte au temps de Saladin et de Richard Coeur de Lion' in Paviot, J. & Verger, J. (eds.), *Guerre, Pouvoir et Noblesse au Moyen Age* (Paris, 2000) pp. 503–11

Milwright, M., 'Reynald of Châtillon and the Red Sea Expedition of 1182–83' in Christie, N. & Yazigi, M. (eds.), *Noble Ideals and Bloody Realities: Warfare in the Middle Ages* (Leiden, 2006) pp. 235–59

Mohring, H. (tr. Bachrach, D. S.), *Saladin: The Sultan and his Times 1138–1193* (Baltimore, 2008)

Mouton, J-M. (et al.), *Sadr: Une forteresse de Saladin dans le Sinai* (Paris, 2007)

Mouton, J-M. & Abd al-Malik, S. S, 'La forteresse de l'Isle de Graye (Qal'at Ayla) à l'époque de Saladin', *Annales Islamologiques*, 29 (1995) pp. 75–90

Omran, M. S., 'King Amalric and the Siege of Alexandria, 1167' in Edbury, P. W. (ed.), *Crusade and Settlement* (Cardiff, 1985) pp. 191–96

——, 'Truces between Moslems and Crusaders (1174–1217 AD)' in Balard, M. (ed.), *Autour de la Premiere Croisade* (Paris, 1996) pp. 423–551

Prawer, J., 'La Bataille de Hattin', *Israel Exploration Journal*, 14 (1964) pp. 160–79

Rex Smith, G., *The Ayyubids and Early Rasulids in the Yemen (567–694/1173–1295): Gibb Memorial Series, XXVI/2* (London, 1978)

Richard, J., 'An Account of the Battle of Hattin referring to the Frankish Mercenaries in Oriental Muslim States' in *Speculum*, 27 (1952) pp. 168–77

Richards, D. S., 'A consideration of two sources for the life of Saladin' in *Journal of Semitic Studies*, 25 (1980) pp. 46–65

Saleh, A. H., 'Saladins et les Bédouins d'Egypte' in *Rendiconti della Reale Academia Nazionale dei Lincei, Scienze Morali*, 34 (1979) pp. 349–54

Sivan, E., 'Notes sur la situation des chrétiens a l'epoque ayyubide' in *Revue de l'Histoire des Religions,* 172 (1967) pp. 117–30

Talmon-Heller, D., 'Islamic Preaching in Syria during the Counter-Crusade (Twelfth-Thirteenth Centuries)' in Shagrir, I. (et al. eds.), *In Laudem Hierosolymitani* (Aldershot, 2007) pp. 61–75

Tolan, J. V., 'Mirror of Chivalry: Salah al-Din in the Medieval European Imagination' in *Cairo Papers in Social Science*, 19 (1996) pp. 7–38

Wieczorek, A. (et al. eds.), *Saladin und die Kreuzfahrer* (Mainz, 2005)

Zouache, A., *Armées et combats en Syrie (491/1098–569/1174)* (Damascus, 2008)

GLOSSARY

'abid   a slave, either in a civilian or a military capacity.

Asadiyah   the regiment recruited and paid by Saladin's uncle, Asad al-Din Shirkuh.

atabeg   originally an advisor to a young ruler, subsequently a local ruler or governor, literally 'father to the prince'.

caliph   successor to the Prophet Muhammad as temporal leader of the Islamic community, but *not* having the Prophet's religious authority except in terms of interpreting what the Prophet had revealed to the Muslim community.

caliphate   both the state ruled by a caliph, and the role, status or 'job' of the caliph.

conrois   medieval French term for a close-packed cavalry formation.

dinar   high-value gold coin in the Islamic world.

dirham   low-value coin, usually copper or silver, in the Islamic world.

diwan   government department or office.

furusiyya   'horsemanship', encompassing riding and combat skills as well as the 'chivalric' attitudes associated with them.

Hadith   saying attributed to the Prophet Muhammad.

Hajj   Islamic pilgrimage to Mecca.

'iqta   source of revenue, usually in the form of a land allocation.

Jazira   literally 'island', referring to the area between the rivers Tigris and Euphrates (ancient Mesopotamia).

kazaghand   mail-lined and padded body armour.

khan   refuge for merchant caravans, sometimes fortified.

madrasah   Islamic school, usually attached to a mosque.

mamluk   soldier of slave-recruited origin.

manshur   official certificate, often confirming the villages or other territory that would form an *'iqta* fief.

maqamat   collection of stories, usually referring to those written by al-Hariri.

muttawiya   religiously motivated volunteers for jihad warfare.

qubbat   domed building, usually covering a tomb.

Sa'id   the Nile Valley from the southern tip of the Nile Delta to Aswan.

shini   oar-powered warship, galley.

sudani   a person from Bilad al-Sudan, meaning 'land of the blacks', thus normally referring to all sub-Saharan Africans.

umma   the worldwide community of Islam.

wazir   senior government minister, vizier.

zariba   field fortification made of available brushwood, thorn bushes, etc.

INDEX